PRAISE FOR *CHANGE THE NARRATIVE*

M000209091

With the world at a breaking
breath of fresh air in the form
schools in a positive direction.
antiracist leaders demonstrate equitable leadership, which is a concept we all can rally behind. Jam-packed with practical strategies,
any leader regardless of their experiences will benefit from this
resource.

—**Eric Sheninger,** best-selling author and keynote speaker

Turner and Lopes strike a balance of coaching and patience, reflection and risk-taking, moral imperative and concrete strategies.
There is no doubt that this text, brilliantly researched and woven
with their personal stories, will help readers reimagine their schools
and evolve their practice.

—**Katie Novak,** author of *UDL Now* and *Equity by Design*

If something in your gut tells you that the #bancrt movement further disadvantages populations that have been traditionally disad-
vantaged, *Change the Narrative* will arm you with tools to understand
the need to actively support all our students. *Change the Narrative* is
a must-read for any educator preparing to confront structural barriers with awareness, empathy, and cultural competency.

—**Hedreich Nichols von Reichert,** author, educator,
and founder of SmallBites

Overflowing with critical analysis, situational training scenarios,
empirical research, and life-altering liberation pedagogy, *Change the
Narrative* gives educators the courage, insight, and direction to stay
accountable in making antiracism in school leadership a standard,
not an aspiration.

—**Grant Hightower,** director of community and
equity, Concord Academy

I found myself both nodding in agreement and tilting my head
deep in thought as I read. In all of the reading and listening I have
done, there was something missing before, and I'm grateful that the
gap has been filled for educators who are eagerly looking for an

action-oriented, research-based approach to doing antiracist work in their school communities.

—**Kerry Gallagher,** assistant principal for teaching and learning, St. John's Prep, and education director, ConnectSafely

Turner and Lopes have written a must-read for any school leader seeking to establish and/or sustain antiracist school culture through the use of practical, sequential yet iterative, easy-to-follow steps that guide readers to the intersection of grace and accountability for the sake of all students, staff, and families.

—**Devin Morris,** cofounder and executive director, The Teachers' Lounge

Since the inception of our nation, racism has permeated all aspects of society, including all levels of our school systems. Creating a culture of anitiracism takes bold, unapologetic leadership, and *Change the Narrative* will help educators first look inward to examine their own mindsets and practices, and then look outward to make the needed changes to the system as a whole. Every child needs and deserves a school experience where they are seen, included, and valued, and Turner and Lopes have created this dynamic resource to help you do just that!

—**Thomas C. Murray,** director of innovation, Future Ready Schools

Through their own personal and professional experience as antiracist educators, Turner and Lopes recognize the important components of this work in schools: the internal reflection and the external action that create socially conscious educational communities that keep students centered and provide agency to historically marginalized and silenced groups.

—**Johnny Cole,** director of equity and student support, Lexington Public Schools

A few PD sessions on equity and antiracism are not going to create the schools that our students, staff, and communities need. We need a continuous cycle of learning, reflection, action, and assessment to truly change the narrative and dismantle the systemic inequities we have inherited. Henry and Kathy explore this cycle in depth, with resources to support leaders, staff, students, and community members.

—Patrick Larkin, assistant superintendent,
Burlington Public Schools

Often, principals and educational leaders wonder what specific and actionable steps can be taken presently to grow their own culturally responsive learning community or educational system. *Change the Narrative* offers a pathway toward promoting the personal and professional transformation needed in order to establish effective antiracist leadership as well as equitable and inclusive practice across the PK–12 setting.

—Dr. Sujan "Suzie" Talukdar, antiracist instructional leader
and school principal

Our schools and institutions need educators and leaders who are courageous enough to acknowledge the role race plays as a barrier to learning. Our learning environments are not universally designed if we lack the willingness to address race, racism, and the need for culturally responsive, antiracist practices and culture. Turner and Lopes not only acknowledge this, they provide readers with tools that are necessary to engage in the work of changing the narrative.

—Mirko Chardin, chief equity and inclusion officer,
Novak Education

In *Change the Narrative*, Turner and Lopes highlight challenges to creating inclusive and equitable learning environments and provide a powerful framework to engage in critical conversations to work collaboratively and create meaningful change.

—Katie Martin, author of *Evolving Education*

The authors have provided a playbook for how to structure conversations and plans for action that are centered around racism. This book is an asset for equity work in every school. It is a bold, brave, and groundbreaking tool that will ignite change in public education.

—Bethany Hill, teacher retention and recruitment specialist

CHANGE THE NARRATIVE

CHANGE
THE NARRATIVE

HOW TO FOSTER AN ANTIRACIST CULTURE IN YOUR SCHOOL

HENRY J. TURNER & KATHY LOPES

CHANGE
THE NARRATIVE

Change the Narrative: How to Foster an Antiracist Culture in Your School
© 2022 Henry J. Turner and Kathy Lopes

All rights reserved. No part of this publication may be reproduced in any form or by any electronic or mechanical means, including information storage and retrieval systems, without permission in writing by the publisher, except by a reviewer who may quote brief passages in a review. For information regarding permission, contact the publisher at books@daveburgessconsulting.com.

This book is available at special discounts when purchased in quantity for educational purposes or for use as premiums, promotions, or fundraisers. For inquiries and details, contact the publisher at books@daveburgessconsulting.com.

Published by Dave Burgess Consulting, Inc.
San Diego, CA
DaveBurgessConsulting.com

Library of Congress Control Number: 2022935909
Paperback ISBN: 978-1-956306-21-7
Ebook ISBN: 978-1-956306-22-4

Cover design by Emily Mahon
Interior design by Liz Schreiter
Edited and produced by Reading List Editorial
ReadingListEditorial.com

To the educators of color who show up every day for all of your students and inspire a narrative of possibilities.

CONTENTS

FOREWORD

In a society that tucks away the truth and hides its history well, there is dire need for truth-tellers. We cannot be content with simply unearthing new information that confirms that which we believed to be true; rather, we need bold voices on the frontlines that will challenge and encourage us all to work toward changing the narrative. This book strips us of any excuses for not knowing the *what, why,* and *how* of creating an antiracist school culture. As Lopes and Turner say, "To be antiracists, we need to own that we are part of the system that upholds such advantages and disadvantages based on race." This applies to all of us!

Through concrete examples, tools, and activities that make the text applicable and accessible to educators at all grade levels and at all points in their antiracist development, the authors provide practical guidance for how to build a school culture rooted in racial equity and culturally responsive instruction. In one powerful example, they recount a time when teachers of color shared their frustrations about professional development in race and racism that was too basic for their own experience. "The next year," they write, "[Turner] worked with faculty members of color to design workshops and to differentiate the professional development structure so that educators could engage at different levels based on their own comfort with issues of race."

For many school leaders, there may be a temptation to keep it kind and keep it simple when it comes to discussing race. While this may sound good in theory, are we simply killing our students softly with such an approach, particularly our students of color? Lopes and Turner state a hard truth: "Colorblind leadership has been the norm for years, and the results are that we punish, fail, and ignore the unique mental health needs of BIPOC students. We then wonder why these subgroups feel disproportionately more disconnected and drop out."

Engaging in reflection is a necessary, however uncomfortable, practice that can inspire growth. *Changing the Narrative* is not for passive leaders. It is an ongoing call to action for those who are ready to dismantle and disrupt. While Lopes and Turner do not pretend to have all the answers, they offer invaluable insight and a practical approach to doing what many of us claim we want to do: build and sustain antiracist schools.

We are in a time where antiracist leadership in schools is more necessary than ever. We don't have the luxury of depending on individual teachers' antiracist lessons and units alone. We need school leaders who prioritize antiracist schools, culture, teaching, learning, and approaches. And we need administrators who are ready to engage in the hands-on work of designing professional development and cultivating school- and districtwide practices that will lead to equitable schools for all students.

Lorena and Roberto Germán
Co-founders, Multicultural Classroom
Tampa, Florida
multiculturalclassroom.com

INTRODUCTION

I t was one of those energizing moments at Newton North High School, when alumni returned for a visit and, as educators, we got a small glimpse into the impact of our labor. When students graduate and go off into their continued journey of self-discovery, we aren't always able to know what lessons they take with them or what values they'll uphold when they are met with challenges. These moments aren't frequent, but when they happen they are worth celebrating—as Henry did that day on social media with his favorite hashtag: #proudprincipal.

That morning, ten recent graduates returned to their high school to speak on a panel to current students about their college experiences. This annual event was hosted by a student academic affinity group that creates a community for high-achieving Black and Latinx students to come together in solidarity and in response to stereotypical myths and negative narratives about the earnestness and capacity of Black and brown students in education.

As the number of students who have joined this group has increased over the years, these students have increasingly connected with one another and become more vocal within their schools. This leadership was demonstrated by each of the alumni on the panel that day, which included students who were attending Ivy League schools, Historically Black Colleges and Universities (HBCUs), small and large state universities and colleges all over the United States. This event was specifically designed for students to hear how alumni were navigating their college experiences as fellow Black, Indigenous, and people of color (BIPOC)[1] students and, for some, as the first person in their family to go to college. Yet it was only a few years earlier these college and university students had sat in the same seats as the current students, listening to other returning college students share their experiences.

During the panel, many of the alumni, particularly those who attended predominantly white institutions (PWI), spoke about the "imposter syndrome" they felt when they arrived on campus. They questioned whether they were as good as the other students they were meeting for the first time, or if, as students of color, they would underperform or drop out in line with the racial disparities that exist in majority white colleges throughout the United States. Many of them spoke about the academic and social justice skills they had learned at Newton North that prepared them to challenge these feelings of imposter syndrome.[2]

One student, (we will call her "Lamari" for the sake of anonymity), shared a story about her experience taking a statistics course as a freshman in a large lecture hall at her large public university and how imposter syndrome showed up for her in a statistics class among white peers. Social psychology research shows that, during an activity, stereotype threat negatively impacts people in a particular group when a stereotype exists that their group doesn't perform as well in that activity as the dominant group.[3] In fact, stereotype threat negatively impacts the highest-performing people of those groups the most. Therefore, Lamari's imposter syndrome in this statistics class was understandable when the stereotype for women and for Black people is that they are less capable than male and white and Asian students. As a Black woman, the stereotype Lamari dealt with was doubly challenging in this course.

---

1 Note that we use *BIPOC* and *people* or *students of color* interchangeably.

2 According to the National Center for Education Statistics, PWIs graduate 78 percent of Black students despite enrolling 87 percent of Black students. This study demonstrated the higher rate of graduation at HBCUs. Kevin S. McClain and April Perry, "Where Did They Go: Retention Rates for Students of Color at Predominantly White Institutions," *College Student Affairs Leadership* 4, no. 1 (2017): 3.

3 To read more about stereotype threat, see Claude M. Steele, *Whistling Vivaldi: How Stereotypes Affect Us and What We Can Do* (New York: W. W. Norton & Company, 2011).

She went on to share how despite these imposed feelings of inadequacy, she felt her high school experience had prepared her academically and given her self-confidence. She later wound up tutoring a group of white male classmates. Because of her understanding of racism, she recognized the importance of that moment. As she was sharing her story, she confidently stated, "I realized that I was just as capable as anyone in my school." "YES!" Henry remembered screaming as he looked on at Lamari and the rest of the students as a proud educator.

Lamari was grateful to her high school AP Statistics teacher for giving her the confidence and knowledge to prepare her to not only excel in her college statistics class but to be able to tutor other students. It is true that Lamari's success in AP Statistics and her partnership with her teacher were very important. However, there are other critical pieces to take from this narrative of confidence, efficacy, and agency.

Just a few years prior, as a high school student, Lamari had participated in this same academic affinity group, as well as other affinity groups, such as a Black student-led group. She was a social justice leader in her school community, leading a rally at the school after students used racist slurs on social media and helping lead a march of more than 1,000 students in support of Black Lives Matter. She worked with teachers and counselors who were "warm demanders," as Zaretta Hammond writes in *Culturally Responsive Teaching and the Brain*, who made sure that Lamari knew they both cared about her and maintained high expectations for her, as well.[4] Her teachers incorporated culturally relevant pedagogy and worked with her to develop social justice skills, such as expressing pride in her own identity, understanding the power and privilege of other identities, and taking action against bias and injustice.

Lamari also learned about historical and modern forms of racism so that when she was confronted with this moment of tutoring a group of white males in her statistics class, she understood the

---

4 Zaretta Hammond, *Culturally Responsive Teaching and the Brain: Promoting Authentic Engagement and Rigor Among Culturally and Linguistically Diverse Students* (Thousand Oaks, CA: Corwin, 2015).

hurdles she was overcoming so that she would persevere through her imposter syndrome.

The narrative about Lamari is one of empowerment. Similar narratives showed up in every story from the students on this panel, and the connection and validation were palpable to the hundred current students in the room. Their shared story is that they attended a high school that was committed to forming an antiracist culture, in a district that was committed to racial justice. While not immune to racism, these students demonstrated that a commitment to antiracism supports the success of students in marginalized groups. But antiracism is not just about these students. Rather, antiracist cultures benefit all students, because these cultures believe that all students thrive in a learning environment that 1) understands the inequities that exist due to racist structures and systems, 2) commits to dismantling racism so that students know their school loves them, and 3) helps students feel empowered to create change so they will excel. This is the narrative that we should be looking for in all our schools. This narrative is possible.

If you picked up this book, then it is likely no secret to you that systemic racism plagues our society, and our schools are not immune. Schools were designed within a racist system, creating disparities in what and how our students learn and normalizing racism; we have to dismantle the systems, policies, practices, and structures that create this inequity. Regardless of whether your school is racially diverse, majority white, or majority students of color, the only way to dismantle racism is to see the role that race plays in our schools and identify racism within it.

This work begins with the individual who is prepared to look within and lead an entire school community in cultivating an antiracist culture. Although this work may begin with the leadership of one person, ultimately it cannot be done alone—it is a collaborative mission that includes everyone in the school community. There are many books on how to help individuals think about becoming antiracist, but rarely do these books expand beyond the individual or provide guidance on how to lead this work within your school structure. This is a practical book for school leaders to learn the steps on how to begin this journey and lead others with an antiracist mindset. As educators who have held numerous positions of leadership, we wholeheartedly believe that good leadership and antiracist leadership is one and the same: To be an effective leader, you must become an antiracist leader. An antiracist leader sees race and acknowledges racism and makes dismantling racism the driving force of their work, using leadership strategies to implement this work. Dismantling racism needs to be at the forefront of leadership, not an afterthought.

Racial Disparities

In 1901, scholar W. E. B. Du Bois predicted that the problem of the twentieth century would be the color line. This statement continues to hold in the third decade of the twenty-first century. Race continues to be one of the most prominent tensions in the United States, although some ignore and deny this fact. Racial disparities in education present some of the most striking problems.

- Discipline rates remain significantly disproportionate between Black and brown students and white students.
- Black students are identified for special education at disproportionate rates compared to white students.
- The school-to-prison pipeline continues to be sustained by harsh zero-tolerance policies.
- Acts of racism have increased in schools across the country.
- One study identified that nearly 10 percent of the almost 10,000 anti-Asian attacks that occurred between March 2020 and September 2021 (the first year and a half of the COVID-19 pandemic) were attacks on youth.[5]

---

5 Aggie J. Yellow Horse et al., *Stop AAPI Hate National Report* (San Francisco: Stop AAPI Hate, 2021).

- American public schools are as diverse as they have ever been, and people of color are quickly becoming the majority in the United States, yet American schools remain segregated. Segregated housing also means most Black and brown families are living in communities with substandard health care, limited access to resources, and underfunded and under-resourced school systems.[6]

These racial disparities indicate the kind of education system students of color experience in comparison to that of white students. These disparities can often be ignored by white communities within individual schools because of the lack of diversity or the small numbers of students of color. From a broader perspective, schools can appear to be performing very well, even when the school is underserving BIPOC students, resulting in disproportionate experiences.

Furthermore, in school communities that are close to 100 percent white, race can be ignored because only a few students of color attend the school. In our experience working with school communities in this category, racial issues can feel distant and therefore be ignored. Even when these school districts attempt to discuss race in their classrooms, they are met with deep resistance from the community and families. These systems contribute to the notion that race is "not our problem" and therefore does not need to be discussed. In these districts, students end up graduating with very little awareness of their racial identity and unable to engage in conversations about race as adults.

---

6 Some resources for statistics about racial disparities in schools include: UNCF, *K-12 Disparity Facts and Statistics*, uncf.org/pages/k-12-disparity-facts-and-stats; Stop AAPI Hate, stopaapihate. org/; Kirsten Weir, "Inequality at School," *Monitor on Psychology* 47, no. 10 (November 2016), apa.org/monitor/2016/11/cover-inequality-school; Kenneth Shores et al., "Categorical Inequalities between Black and White Students Are Common in US Schools—But They Don't Have to Be," *Brown Center Chalkboard*, The Brookings Institution, February 21, 2020, brookings. edu/blog/brown-center-chalkboard/2020/02/21/categorical-inequalities-between-black-and -white-students-are-common-in-us-schools-but-they-dont-have-to-be/; Adam Voight et al., "The Racial School Climate Gap: Within-School Disparities in Students' Experiences of Safety, Support, and Connectedness," *American Journal of Community Psychology* 56, no. 3–4 (December 2015): 252–267.

The American school system has been structurally the same since the nineteenth century—working on a bell system, all students sitting in desks most of the time, teacher-centered instruction—as well as the tendency to accept as truth that these structures cannot be changed. As educators we accept this falsehood that systemic change is not possible and so focus on changes around the margins. When we attempt to make systemic change, we are forced to cave to the demands of our most empowered families and further marginalize those students who have been historically marginalized. Teachers become frustrated with the lack of progress and choose to go their own path in their classroom. When we accept the status quo, we do so with a colorblind and power-blind perspective that suggests all students have equal opportunity to thrive in our schools. We accept that the racial disparities that exist in the American school system are our students' fault and not ours or our schools'. We need to change the narrative.

The purpose of this book is to help school leaders change the narrative of our schools through the lens of antiracism so that all students, regardless of race, can thrive. The path to this new narrative is a school where all students feel empowered and engaged so that they can succeed. When we look at the students who currently excel in our schools, they do so because they obtain power and privilege from a school system inherently designed for them. These students are able to navigate school fluidly, with courses designed with them in mind and teaching practices designed to allow them to access and comprehend materials.

The question for all educators around racism in our schools is: "What are you doing to dismantle it?" Having grown up and worked within majority white schools as people of color, we have experienced a range of responses from educators about the disparities that exist in our schools and our communities. While educators of color are called on to lead workshops and training, many white educators can often choose to disengage. At the root of this, we see a disconnect in one's willingness to be reflective of their own identity in connection to race and racism. Racism is at the root of our country and permeates all aspects of our society. We have been taught that our history is one of exceptionalism and freedom. But it is also true that our country's history has been one of oppression and inequity. Those of us who have experienced this oppression—people of color, immigrants, women, members of the LGBTQ+ community, and others—can understand that we have a history of struggling to attain this freedom. And yet, groups who are able to obtain this freedom are taught to ignore the oppression that exists for others.

Why We Wrote This Book

We wrote this book for two reasons. First, we want to help educators lead in this work. There is a lot of writing and training to support educators in developing their own racial identity and creating an antiracist classroom. While this literature is very important in spaces where educators feel like they are on their own in this work, racism will persist until antiracism is a part of a school's culture and until the majority of the school community is working to dismantle racism. The time is now. We believe there is an energized commitment by many white people to address systemic racism, but this requires leadership.

Our shared experiences of growing up in predominantly white communities and experiencing our identity development within predominantly white educational and professional spaces—regularly as one of the few, if not only, people of color in the room or at the table—have brought us to where we are today. While we did not know each other at the time of those experiences, we both attended the University of Massachusetts at Amherst, which was formative for us in our racial identity development, as well as our commitment to address racial inequity. Our careers took different paths: Kathy became a social worker and is now director of diversity, equity, and inclusion, and Henry a history teacher and now a high school principal. Despite these differences, our careers have been focused on addressing racial inequity. Each of us has over twenty years of experience working with educators on how to dismantle racism in schools, whether we were with our own colleagues, with other educators at conferences, on social media, or at workshops. With all of this, we came to know each other while working together in the Newton Public Schools in Newton, Massachusetts.

This leads us to our second purpose for writing this book: to help us formulate our own thinking to envision what an antiracist school could look like and how to get there. While we are proud of our work as leaders who foster an antiracist culture in our schools, we have not solved racism in our schools, and as we attack one issue, other issues pop up. Throughout this book you will see examples of work we are proud of, as well as areas we are still working through or hoping to address in the future.

The Structure of the Book

This book is divided into two parts, and each chapter is titled for its particular focus on the path to antiracist leadership.

The first section is focused on how we can understand ourselves as antiracist leaders; it sets the table for what antiracist leadership looks like and provides a model for growing in this work. Through these first five chapters, we emphasize the importance of self-growth as a model for others, but we also help leaders incorporate the cycle of an antiracist school culture. The second section describes how leaders foster an antiracist culture. Using the framework described in the first section, we unpack different components of school culture, from professional development and student life to instruction and supporting families. We want you to use this book to push your thinking as a school leader and we want it to serve as a reference that you can come back to as you pursue fostering an antiracist culture in your school. Antiracism is a mindset, not an end. There is no SMART goal that you can create and check off once you solve racism in your school. You need to pursue this work every moment of every day. We hope this book can be your guide as you dive into this work.

Finally, we keep the term *leader* very general in this book, as we know that every school has a different leadership culture and there are many leaders in every community. We also make a big assumption that you are reading this because you want to join us in the fight against racism in schools. We wrote this for those of you who have been in this struggle for your entire career, as well as those of you who are just starting out on your journey. We are also very specific about who we did not write this book for. If you resist the idea that racial disparities exist in our schools, if you continue to blame kids for their lack of achievement in our schools, if you believe that we should delete topics on race and racism from our curriculum because it makes students feel uncomfortable, and if you reject diversity, equity, and inclusion as important educational concepts—then this book is not for you yet. However, if you do find yourself back here with a realization that racism is still very real in our schools and that we are all responsible for dismantling it, then this book will be here waiting for you.

Now let's change the narrative.

PART I

UNDERSTANDING OURSELVES
AS ANTIRACIST LEADERS

CHAPTER 1

GOOD LEADERSHIP IS ANTIRACIST LEADERSHIP

The beauty of anti-racism is that you don't have to pretend to be free of racism to be an anti-racist. Anti-racism is the commitment to fighting racism wherever you find it, including in yourself. And it's the only way forward.

—IJEOMA OLUO

During a training on antiracist leadership, a school administrator commented that the solutions we were talking about sounded the same as just "good leadership." He went on to ask, "What's the difference between antiracist leadership and 'good' leadership?" It seemed that he was asking, "What is distinct about being an antiracist leader?" The answer to this is clear: antiracist leaders have an antiracist mindset. They have a commitment to dismantling racism through ongoing learning and reflection, deliberate and sustained action, and they make that central to their work. Antiracist leaders wake up every morning with the commitment to tear down this system. Too often we ascribe good leadership to leaders who run smooth, conflict-free organizations: "Everything is quiet, so they must be doing a good job." But these leaders must be avoiding the challenges of equity and race, which is anything but smooth and conflict free. These leaders try to be colorblind and treat all students equally, but being colorblind means ignoring that racism creates inequity for students of color. Whether intentional or not, pretending to be colorblind creates a school culture for the benefit of students with the most privileges. Those who say, "I don't see race," are being unjust to people of color who want to be seen. As people of color, we want to be seen, but not defined by our race.

When race and racism are ignored and avoided, we perpetuate racial disparities in our schools. How many mission statements speak to serving *all* students but are not actually designed to serve all students? Pervasive practices that marginalize BIPOC students and privilege white students perpetuate our existing racist structures. We also believe that although white students benefit from these racist structures, racism ultimately limits their potential for learning. These structures can also hurt other marginalized groups, such as girls, nonbinary students, members of the LGBTQ+ community, and low-income students. Intersectionality helps us understand that students of color who are also a part of these marginalized groups are further hurt.

Colorblind leadership has been the norm for years, and the results are that we punish, fail, and ignore the unique mental health needs of BIPOC students. We then wonder why these subgroups feel disproportionately more disconnected and drop out. As remedies, we place them in special education, force them to come after school and during the summer to do more work, and label them as the cause of the achievement gap. We need, instead, to see the racism that exists in our schools and the impact it has on students of color.

We need to expand our definition of good leadership. We need to understand good leaders as those who commit to taking action to dismantle systemic racism—to being antiracist leaders. This chapter provides a framework for what we mean by "antiracist leadership" and how it is different from what is perceived as "good leadership." We begin with a discussion of what antiracism is and is not before turning to look at how to connect antiracism and leadership. Throughout our discussion, we emphasize the importance of continually returning to the work of antiracism.

Committing to Antiracism

Antiracism is active work that requires self-reflection on one's own racist ideas and contributions to racism. Committing to this work means that leaders are continually evaluating their own role within racism. Doing so requires first understanding what racism is.

Racism and Antiracism

The definition of racism we use comes from David Wellman's *Portraits of White Racism*, which defines racism as "a system of advantage based on race."[1] In the 1990s, Beverly Daniel Tatum reaffirmed this definition in her classic book *Why Are All the Black Kids Sitting Together in the Cafeteria?*, and again in the book's twentieth anniversary edition in 2017.[2] Tatum writes, "This definition of racism is useful because it allows us to see that racism, like other forms of oppression, is not only a personal ideology based on racial prejudice, but a system involving cultural messages and institutional policies and practices as well as beliefs and actions of individuals. In the United States, this system clearly operates to the advantage of whites and to the disadvantage of people of color." Racism is a system we all live within. As a result, many common ideas that we perceive to be "normal" or "traditional" are actually racist ideas. Have we accepted the Native American headdress on the school's mascot as tradition? Have we excused a team's "gangsta" spirit as kids having fun? Do we find relief that no one saw the racist graffiti in the bathroom, so we can erase it and move on with our day? Do we let the majority-white classroom vote as a class whether they should use the N-word in *Huckleberry Finn*? Microaggressions and racist acts can be ignored or justified very easily, particularly when we are the ones involved. This is why it is important that antiracist leaders are self-reflective and assess their own racist ideas.

---

1 David T. Wellman, *Portraits of White Racism* (Cambridge: Cambridge University Press, 1977).

2 Beverly Daniel Tatum, *Why Are All the Black Kids Sitting Together in the Cafeteria?: And Other Conversations about Race*, 20th anniversary ed. (New York: Basic Books, 2017).

What is the difference between racist and antiracist? Using the chart below (figure 1.1), try this activity: While considering the broad categories of "active racist," "passive racist," "active antiracist," and "passive antiracist," discussed below, come up with actions that a person in each category might take. It is worth noting that these terms are fluid and that a person can be racist in one moment and antiracist the next.

Figure 1.1

Passive Racist	Active Racist
Passive Antiracist	Active Antiracist

- **An *active racist* mindset is when someone actively works to uphold the system of advantage based on race**. Attending a white supremacist rally is an example of active racism. But so is the educator who knowingly ignores students' needs to see themselves in literature and instead chooses all white male authors because they represent the "classics," or the educator who refuses to discuss the presence of race in your school, or the coach who uses racist nicknames for their players.
- **A *passive racist* mindset is when a person allows for racism to occur and doesn't act**. Examples of this would be when we allow a racist policy to exist, when we hear a racist joke and do not respond, when we try to take a "colorblind" approach to

providing discipline, when we ignore the impact our grading practices have on students, when we don't consider the cultural needs of a student when it comes to their mental health, or when we enable the parent who doesn't want their child interacting with "those" kids.

- **An *active antiracist* mindset is when a person actively works to dismantle racism.** An active antiracist would be someone who calls out a racist comment, fights to end a racist policy, educates others on how to be an antiracist, incorporates instructional strategies so that students can discuss issues involving race in current events, or joins the diversity, equity, and inclusion committee to unpack the systemic racism that exists in the school.
- **A *passive antiracist* mindset?** Can you think of an example? No? The purpose of this activity is to see that antiracists are actively working to dismantle racism, there is no way to sit idly by. When we don't do anything, we are acting as passive racists. There is no such thing as a passive antiracist.

Acknowledging Our Own Contributions to Racism

Ibram X. Kendi's *How to Be an Antiracist* demonstrates how the term *racist* is not a pejorative, but simply a description of when we are working to dismantle racist ideas and policies, and when we are not.[3] It is helpful to think about this concept—that *racist* is not a pejorative term—because believing that it is can lead to a fixed mindset that we are either racist or not, instead of to reflection on our own actions that support this system of advantage. Thinking about the activity above, we may find ourselves in one moment landing in the passive racist category, and in the next moment in the antiracist category. We are not fixed racist or antiracist. Rather, the question is, are we learning to become conscious that racism is a "system of advantage based on race"

---

3 Ibram X. Kendi, *How to Be an Antiracist* (New York: One World, 2019).

and of when we are demonstrating passive or active racism versus antiracism? When we become aware of our actions, we then choose actions that are active in dismantling this system.

Kendi also writes in the book, "The opposite of racist isn't 'not racist.' It is 'antiracist.' What's the difference? One either endorses the idea of a belief in racial hierarchy as a racist, or in racial equality as an antiracist. One either believes as a racist that problems are rooted in groups of people, or, as an antiracist, locates the roots of problems in power and policies. One either allows racial inequities to persevere as a racist, or confronts racial inequities as an antiracist. There is no in-between safe space of 'not racist.' " Furthermore, Kendi centers his book around his own contributions to upholding racism. By doing so, he points to the fact that we can all have racist ideas or uphold racist policies. An antiracist is not defined as someone who does not hold racist ideas—a near impossibility in the confines of our racist society— but rather as someone who is committed to this work of dismantling racist ideas and policies in every moment of every day. This is a tall task, and we are likely to fail to live up to this high expectation. This is why antiracism is lifelong work, and work that we must always come back to.

If we ignore the role we play as either racists or antiracists in day-to-day interactions, then we cannot dismantle the system of racism. When, as educators, we say that we care about equity but look only at structures outside of our control, then we are doing nothing to solve the problem. For example, it is easy to say, "Our society needs to fix the prison system." But it is far more challenging to consider the actions and policies that we have direct control over, such as how we engage students in school, our grading policies, and our disciplinary practices. These three factors are used as predictors for a student's success after high school. In fact, according to the Brookings Institute, there is a 70 percent chance that an African American man without a high school diploma will be incarcerated by his mid-thirties.[4] To be antiracists, we need to own that we are part of the system that upholds such advantages and disadvantages based on race.

As we reflect on our own contributions to racism and commit to an antiracist mindset it is important to understand that this work is hard and requires a commitment every moment of every day. Often when we first learn about antiracism, we are inspired to make an immediate change. The problem is that racism is an all-encompassing and long-standing system that we have been accustomed to accepting as normal. Therefore, to believe that certain policies or practices will solve racism is misguided. While one can have an antiracist mindset in one moment, it is much harder to maintain an antiracist mindset every moment of every day.

Understanding Our Bias

The work of educators is fast paced, stressful, and exhausting, and we are often forced to multitask because of this dynamic in schools. As a result of this multitasking and quick thinking, it is likely that our implicit bias regularly clouds our decision-making.

We have seen many examples of how police officers' unconscious bias shows up in stops, use of excessive force, and murders of BIPOC. While teachers do not typically face life-or-death situations at work, our own unconscious bias has a significant effect on the academic success of our students. Decisions around discipline, grading, and levels of class rigor often result in outcomes that reinforce our unconscious biases regarding which types of students do well in school and which types of students do not succeed. This is exacerbated when we defend our practices as being "in the best interest of the student." How often have we heard that a suspension is necessary because it will help

---

4   For more on this topic check out Melissa S. Kearney and Benjamin H. Harris, *Ten Economic Facts about Crime and Incarceration in the United States* (Washington, DC: The Brookings Institution, 2014), brookings.edu/research/ten-economic-facts-about-crime-and-incarceration -in-the-united-states/.

a student learn from their mistakes? We justify our behavior in the same way a police officer justifies their decisions in ensuring safety in a community.

As a result of our own bias as educators, racial disparities permeate our schools. Figure 1.2 shows these disparities for several key indicators for all BIPOC students compared to white students. While disparities for Black and Native American students are consistently high in many categories, it is important to understand the disparities that exist due to racism for all students. For example, it is important to understand the racism that exists for Asian students. For example, 16 percent of hate incidents self-reported to the organization Stop AAPI Hate during the summer of 2020 were from youth.[5] It is clear that this crisis will have an even greater impact on the mental health disparity for Asian students.[6] Acknowledging that our structures and policies are the problem is an antiracist act.

Figure 1.2 Examples of Racial Disparities in Schools (percentage)

	Asian	Black	Latinx	Multi-racial	Native American	Pacific Islander	White
Suspension rate (2019)	1.1	13.7	4.5	5.3	6.7	4.5	3.4
Expulsion	>.1	.4	.1	.3	.4	.1	.2

---

5 Megan Dela Cruz et al., *They Blamed Me because I Am Asian: Findings from Youth-Reported Incidents of Anti-AAPI Hate* (San Francisco: Stop AAPI Hate, 2020), stopaapihate.org/wp-content/uploads/2021/04/Stop-AAPI-Hate-Report-Youth-Campaign-200917.pdf.

6 Koko Nishi, "Mental Health Among Asian-Americans," *Students' Corner*, American Psychological Association, 2012, apa.org/pi/oema/resources/ethnicity-health/asian-american/article-mental-health#:~:text=Recent%20data%20collected%20from%20the,mental%20health%20services%20than%20Whites.

	Asian	Black	Latinx	Multi-racial	Native American	Pacific Islander	White
Percentage of students receiving special education services	7	16	12	13	17	12	14
High school completion rates	97	92	89	96	75	84	94

Source: *Status and Trends in the Education of Racial and Ethnic Groups*, National Center for Education Statistics, updated February 2019, nces.ed.gov/programs/raceindicators/index.asp

Like teachers, police officers have very stressful, high-pressure jobs. Stanford professor Jennifer Eberhardt researches the consequences of unconscious bias in police officers. In her work with the Oakland Police Department, she developed a checklist to slow down officers' thinking before they stop someone, reducing the number of stops among marginalized groups such as African Americans.[7] Perhaps similar protocols would be effective for educators when we make decisions about special education identification or discipline. Additionally, we could use such protocols to slow down teacher thinking when calling on a student in class or when reprimanding a student for perceived misbehavior. There are many options here for leaders to engage with educators to develop structures that slow down our thinking. Activities like the implicit bias test demonstrate that we cannot control bias in our reactionary responses.[8] Our work, therefore, needs to begin with acceptance of our bias and a desire to address it, and we need to buy into structures and systems that help us slow down and reflect.

---

7 Jennifer L. Eberhardt, *Biased: Uncovering the Hidden Prejudice that Shapes What We See, Think, and Do* (New York: Penguin, 2020).

8 If you would like to assess your bias, take the Implicit Association Test: implicit.harvard.edu/implicit/user/agg/blindspot/indexrk.htm.

Leading in a Racist System

As antiracist leaders, we need to ensure that our traditionally marginalized groups are empowered and have a voice. We also need to be vulnerable enough to take feedback from these groups and implement their recommendations for change. A few years ago, during a meeting, the faculty of color affinity group told Henry that whole-school discussions on race were basic and an insult to them. One teacher said, "Whenever we talk about race, it is clearly for white teachers. We have to explain basic concepts every time, and I am constantly bored. It feels almost disrespectful." Henry remembers walking out of that meeting feeling frustrated. He drove home yelling, "Why don't *they* run the meetings!" As many leaders have experienced before, the answer was right in front of his face—he was power-hoarding at meetings. The next year, he worked with faculty members of color to design workshops and to differentiate the professional development structure so that educators could engage at different levels based on their own comfort with issues of race.

Distributed leadership is an effective lens through which to address power-hoarding in our roles as school leaders. Antiracist school leaders need to constantly reflect on our practice and make sure we are collaborating with others and empowering them to make decisions. We also need to empower groups such as faculty, parent organizations, and student groups to challenge our decisions and to take the lead. The only way we can dismantle racism is to create a more inclusive leadership style that challenges a power-hoarding cultural dynamic. Most of the effective leadership and educational strategies that we know work, such as collaborative leadership, professional learning communities, and universal design for learning, while not inherently antiracist, can be used to dismantle racism and affirm more equitable schools.

Antiracist Leadership

The antiracist mindset acknowledges that racism exists in all facets of our society. The work needs to occur outside our schools, as well as in the complex day-to-day happenings of school. Figure 1.3 demonstrates the many different facets that antiracist leaders must dive into if they are to be authentically committed to the work of creating a culture of antiracism in our schools. As described in the examples below, antiracism is not just about one aspect of our work but about the entirety of our work. If this antiracist work is authentic work, then it is personal as much as it is professional.

Figure 1.3 The Systems of an Antiracist Educator

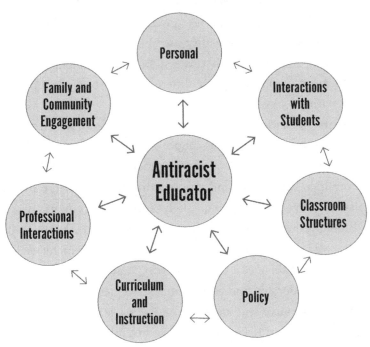

Personal

- Fighting to dismantle racism in other facets of life outside of work.

Interactions with Students

- The school community empowers the voices of students of color to ensure equity.

Classroom Structures

- All students feel loved, safe, and empowered to be their true selves.

Family and Community Engagement

- The voices of families of color are amplified by the school.

Curriculum and Instruction

- Leaders provide clear vision and a professional learning environment that is focused on culturally responsive teaching and culturally relevant content.

Professional Interactions

- White staff members are cognizant of the balance of amplifying the voices of colleagues of color and empowering them to speak of their own accord, as well.

Policy

- Discipline policies address systemic racism and bias.

This list demonstrates how varied and complex antiracist work is—which can feel quite overwhelming—and reinforces that antiracist work is long-term work. Successfully making shifts in some of these areas can take years. The list also demonstrates that a person cannot do this work alone. Therefore, leaders must focus on long-term, sustainable leadership centered on collaboration with and empowerment of others. Antiracist leadership must combine self-work and helping others to do the same.

Commitment to the Long Term

The previous section demonstrates the complexity and interconnectedness of racism in our schools. It should also prove that there is no silver-bullet policy that is going to end racism in our schools. Rather, we must always come back to the understanding that antiracist work is lifelong work and requires commitment every moment of every day. Because one can have an antiracist mindset one moment and a racist one the next, we need to establish a process that allows us to stay in this work at all times.

Inquiry learning is a learning process that allows us to remain self-focused in our growth. While there are many different cycles for inquiry learning, such as 5 E's, Evolving Learner, and Impact Cycle, and each has its own nuance, what they all share is a commitment to following the steps of the cycle and a recognition that the cycle is continuous. This continuous loop is consistent with the growth of an antiracist leader. In consideration of what is required to commit to leading with an antiracist mindset, we developed a cycle to help you to stay in the work and able to tackle different levels of action.

This cycle prevents us from moving too quickly into action. For example, educators who enter this work often get so excited that they want to act right after reading a book on antiracism. In our experience, paths like this always end in failure. Creating change too quickly and without proper consideration can have negative consequences for students, tends not to be collaborative, and is too challenging to achieve alone. The cycle we created incorporates a period of critical reflection, allowing leaders time to process what was learned and to develop a strategy for action.

This cycle also ensures that we are assessing the impact of our actions. Antiracist work is messy because it involves talking about a topic that many people have been trained not to talk about and taking down a system that we have all been brought up in. Mistakes will be made and emotions will be triggered in this work. Additionally, our actions come with many risks, whether it is the political risk of angering a vocal constituency or the potential for failure that comes with any attempt to innovate.

Furthermore, when we engage in challenging actions, such as changing a policy or practice, we need to ensure we are dismantling racism and not reinforcing it. There are many examples of changes that were intended to be antiracist, but instead created further inequity. Oftentimes, these actions are merely performative and fail to have any real impact. Lasting positive impact requires antiracist leadership that is thoughtful and deliberate. For example, we have seen these unchecked intentions backfire when educators lower expectations for students of color because they feel bad for them. We have worked in and with school districts that participate in the Metropolitan Council for Educational Opportunity (METCO)—the largest voluntary desegregation program in the United States. In this program, students of color from Boston get up very early in the morning to take a bus to a majority white suburban school. In our long history with these schools, we have come across educators who allow Boston students to sleep through class because the educator is worried about their lack of sleep. Now, sleep is very important for students; however, letting students sleep through class is not the solution to this problem. We need to develop solutions that dismantle disparities, not reinforce them.

Despite the messiness of this work, committing to a cycle of inquiry will help you to engage in it deliberately and to understand its impact, allowing you to make adjustments along the way. In recognition of the long-term effort involved, the cycle we have found most helpful is designed to support the work's longevity. It is: **Learn-Reflect-Act-Assess.**

This cycle, outlined in figure 1.4, can be used by a leader as they think about their own growth and by a school community as they collectively try to develop an antiracist culture. The remainder of the book details how you can engage in this cycle with different members of the school community. For now, we offer a quick summary of each step and why we incorporated it.

Figure 1.4 Cycle of Learning for the Antiracist Leader

Inspired by Evolving Learner Model[9]

- **Learn:** This is the first step of the cycle and the step you should always return to after the cycle is completed. This step forces you to learn more about racism as well as your own role within the racist system. Learning can come from what we discover about our own racial identity development; data we investigate around racial disparity or the impact of a previous action;

---

9 Lainie Rowell, Kristy Andre, and Lauren Steinmann, *Evolving Learner: Shifting from Professional Development to Professional Learning from Kids, Peers, and the World* (Thousand Oaks, CA: Corwin, 2020).

listening to people of color about their experiences in our schools or larger society; or from questioning an established policy, idea, or structure. This step requires active listening.

- **Reflect**. This step prevents us from moving too quickly to action after our learning. With this step we should make sense of what we've learned and how it impacts our work or the culture of the school. This is a critical step missed by many and may be the reason so many initiatives end up creating more inequity. Reflection happens when we meditate and find space to separate ourselves from our learning; when we journal and write to process what we've learned; when we develop a strategy for our actions; and when we synthesize and make meaning of what we hear from communities of color.

- **Act**. Whether action needs to be immediate or based on strategic thinking, action that follows this cycle is deliberate and focused on dismantling racism and supporting communities of color. Action can take the form of the changes we lead, initiatives we engage in, the policies that are dismantled, and the new curriculum and instruction strategies created.

- **Assess**. This step allows us to monitor and understand the progress and success of our actions. These steps should inform learning and lead us back to the beginning of the cycle. These assessments can be done through audits, surveys, evaluations, checks for learning, and other forms of analysis.

Depending on the work, each step of the cycle will take different amounts of time. For example, a leader could spend a day learning about their racial identity development but be stuck in the learning phase for a year during an equity audit. What is important is that you move through these steps with purpose, focused on dismantling racism and aware of the long road this work takes. To help you along your journey, at the end of every chapter, we provide relevant examples of the four steps in this cycle.

Conclusion

Understanding that antiracism is a mindset to dismantle racist structures and ideas, Dr. Bettina Love explained that "too often we think the work of fighting oppression is just intellectual. The real work is personal, emotional, spiritual, and communal."[10] This work is hard, and it is a lifelong commitment. As people who have committed to this work for a long time, it continues to feel hard. But it's important to begin to understand that antiracism is a lifelong commitment.

As school leaders, our work to dismantle racism is complex because it is embedded in all facets of our work. Therefore, this work should start slowly and should begin with your own personal journey as an antiracist. As you make this commitment, you can then be a model for the rest of your school community, which will begin the creation of an antiracist culture. Using the Antiracist Leader Learning Cycle, chapters 2 through 5 will help you as you begin this journey to becoming an antiracist leader.

KEY IDEAS

- Good school leaders commit to the definition of racism as "a system of advantage based on race" and recognize that it exists in their school.
- Antiracist work is active work that requires self-reflection on one's own contributions to racist systems and a commitment to dismantling racism.
- Antiracist actions require systemic overhauls, not just simple gimmicks. This requires time and constant work.

---

10 Bettina L. Love, *We Want to Do More than Survive: Abolitionist Teaching and the Pursuit of Educational Freedom* (Boston: Beacon Press, 2019).

CHANGE THE NARRATIVE

LEARN–Walk through the active/passive racist versus antiracist activity to learn more about how to be active in interrupting and dismantling racism in the moment.

REFLECT–Think about your leadership style and if/how it encompasses an antiracist mindset. How have you been active versus passive in dealing with racist language, incidents, and crises?

ACT–Choose one area of practice or policy within your school improvement plan and review it specifically with an antiracist lens. Identify areas that need to be reframed and/or restructured.

ASSESS–Create a routine to review your practices and policies with the inquiry cycle of learn-reflect-act-assess.

CHAPTER 2

LEARN

Leadership and learning are indispensable to each other.

—JOHN F. KENNEDY

Now that we have provided a framework for developing antiracist leadership, let's dive a bit deeper into what it means to grow and develop in your personal work as a leader. It begins with the recognition that there continues to be so much to learn—about history, about systems, and about yourself. Many of us landed in leadership roles in our school (formal positions or not) because we worked hard and have skills and personality traits that are attractive to others. Throughout our career we may have received compliments that have given us validation that we are doing a good job and are able to take on more responsibility. Our confidence allows us to show resilience in the face of the criticism we receive in our leadership roles. We are able to "brush things off." When we have success, we can focus on the hard work that it took to get there and forget the privileges we have that have allowed us to move into these roles over others. Even if you are born on third base, you still have to sprint home. And while you feel proud of your hard work, you forget that others are in the batters' box playing with a stick for a bat.

When we ignore that other people were not born on third base, we justify our success. In our society we may be able to understand the inequitable experiences of people we know, such as our family members. For example, if we have a disabled family member, we may recognize the challenges they go through daily. If we are straight and have a gay child, we can learn about the discrimination they endure. When you see the discrimination of people you love, you can easily stand up as an ally. But as we further segregate, too few white people observe the experiences of people outside their personal communities. This is how people of color become othered in a distinct way. Again, when you consider race alongside the intersectionalities of disability, gender, sexual orientation, and other forms of marginalized identity, you can see that people of color who also identify with such traditionally marginalized groups are further discriminated against. A Black, low-SES, trans person with a disability, for example, is going to face more discrimination than a wealthy, heterosexual, Black cisgender male. Nevertheless, the wealthy, heterosexual, Black cisgender male is still discriminated against. Racism is a complex system, so all of this can be true and that is how we need to learn about racism; it exists in all facets of our society, regardless of other privileges. We cannot escape race in a racist system.

Regardless of our identity, we all grew up in a racist system and we need to start our process as antiracist leaders committed to—and open to—learning. As leaders, we have all demonstrated some level of success within this racist system. Regardless of who you are, becoming an effective and transformative leader in antiracism is to embrace that antiracism is an ongoing process of individual and collective choices made with the intent of dismantling systems of oppression. Learning to acknowledge that racism exists begins with the individual's commitment to a lifelong learning process that includes self-reflection, humility, and the unpacking of our values, biases, and actions that contribute to upholding racist structures. It involves deconstructing most of the things we have been taught to believe about fairness and deservedness and hard work, but most importantly, it requires us to hold ourselves accountable.

This chapter provides context for what it means to be a learner who is committed to antiracism and briefly explores some of the critical areas we must learn about. While not comprehensive, what follows provides a good starting point to dive into learning about race and the structures and systems of racism.

Confronting Racism

One of the first, and most important, steps for a school leader is to acknowledge and accept that racism is embedded in all our societal systems and that we have all been indoctrinated to participate in upholding this system, even if unwittingly. In their article "Web of Institutional Racism," social work professors Joshua Miller and Ann Marie Garran describe racism as "painfully obvious to the people of color caught in its strands and yet . . . nearly invisible to many white people who pass through it unimpeded. White people maintain the illusion that many societal institutions, policies, living and working arrangements, programs and organizations are race neutral."[1] The less aware we are of the system, the more we need to commit to learning, which starts with acknowledging and accepting our role within that system and then developing a deeper understanding of whiteness. Being white does not mean that you understand whiteness, because a white supremacist culture perceives whiteness as normal as the "cultural norm" in our society. The section that follows describes how we confront racism by learning about these topics.

---

1 Joshua Miller and Ann Marie Garran, "The Web of Institutional Racism," *Smith College Studies in Social Work* 77, no. 1 (2007): 33–67, doi.org/10.1300/j497v77n01_03.

Acknowledgment and Acceptance

In 2016, The US Department of Education released *The State of Racial Diversity in the Educator Workforce* report,[2] which shared findings that the educator workforce in public schools was overwhelmingly homogeneous, with 82 percent identifying as white. This is in stark contrast to the racial makeup of the student population, with, in 2017, only 48 percent of public school students identifying as white.[3] Because our educational system is staffed overwhelmingly by white leaders and educators, our public school system follows a pattern of white authority. This does not make white educators bad people; rather, we need to acknowledge that we work in a system with perpetual blind spots and bias that ignores the needs of the more diverse student body. We need to acknowledge that we need a more inclusive system with more diverse methods of pedagogy that are representative of diverse cultural norms and committed to dismantling practices and policies harmful toward BIPOC students.

The narrative of racism that most of us adopted through our own educational systems is that it is a personal, individual action that involves overt hate and antagonism toward other races. We were taught to believe racists were bad people. Our genesis of becoming educators allows us to reject the concept that we could support a racist system—we came into this profession to make a difference in the lives of children, so there is no way we can be bad, and therefore we can't be racist. As Ibram Kendi explained, if we move away from the idea that racist is a pejorative and recognize that we can be racist in one moment and not racist the next, we can understand that we all support racism if we do not actively work to end it.

---

2 *The State of Racial Diversity in the Educator Workforce* (Washington, DC: US Department of Education, 2016), www2.ed.gov/rschstat/eval/highered/racial-diversity/state-racial-diversity-workforce.pdf.

3 "Racial/Ethnic Enrollment in Public Schools," *The Condition of Education 2021* (Washington, DC: National Center for Education Statistics, 2021), updated May 2021, nces.ed.gov/programs/coe/indicator/cge.

For a school leader, antiracism means recognizing that your school, as a byproduct of educational structures, is not immune to upholding values of acceptance and success that largely benefit white students, white staff, and white culture. Our hope is that if you are reading this book, you have already arrived at this revelation. This is not about judgment or blame, but a recognition that not all students, staff, and families feel safe or valued in your school community and are therefore not able to access learning in a way that feels equitable and inclusive.

Whiteness, White Supremacy Culture, and Leadership

White supremacy has long been the law and culture of the land. Any attempt to challenge white supremacy has been met with revised laws, cultural backlash, and intimidation and violence. When Black slaves learned to read, violence and laws banning reading were increased. When Black politicians won elections during Reconstruction, voting restrictions and the rise of the Ku Klux Klan terrorized black communities, leading to the creation of Jim Crow. As the civil rights movement dismantled Jim Crow, federal housing policy and white flight created unequal housing, schooling, and overall living conditions for many communities of color. And now as the United States heads toward a majority person of color population, attempts to hinder voting rights and threaten communities of color through domestic terrorism continue to support the maintenance of white supremacy, and schools see laws that prohibit teachers from teaching and talking to their students about racism, and that ban books about racism. All the while, our society blames Black and brown children for creating an achievement gap, accepts police violence against people of color, and calls any policy that attempts to address inequity a handout. When you are white in white America and ignore these patterns of racism, you are only strengthening them.

If this statement makes you feel uncomfortable, good. White supremacy should be a topic you find challenging and frustrating, especially as you begin to recognize the ways it has been embedded in our culture. Whether you are white or a person of color, discussing systemic racism is challenging. When you experience that feeling of discomfort, the worst thing you can do is stop reading or stop learning and inquiring more. The more we understand that the cultural norms in American society are built upon benefiting one race of people and subjugating others, the sooner we can get to a place where we're ready to dismantle that system so that the norms will benefit all.

As a DEI consultant, Kathy has visited numerous schools through-out Massachusetts to deliver workshops and presentations to school leaders and faculty. In the context of this role and as a Black woman, she becomes attuned to the cultural environments of every school she enters. One of the ways she gauges how welcoming and inclusive a school may feel to students and families of color is by how she is acknowledged and greeted when entering a school building for the first time, as well as the setup and design of the main lobby and front office—these being the first places visitors tend to go.

During a visit to a school for a professional development work-shop, she was immediately met with a large wall in the front lobby with oversized pictures of past principals, acknowledging their years of service—all of whom were white men. When she used the exam-ple of this wall and why it may unintentionally convey a relationship between white men and leadership and power, and therefore may not be inclusive or welcoming to all, she was met with resistance. The majority-white educators felt she was being disrespectful of past lead-ers they held in high regard.

In this interaction, what stood out to Kathy was their inability to hear her perspective as one that was true to her experience and worthy of contemplation. In that moment (and in many moments), the needs and values of the dominant group—white educators—were centered and prioritized. Kathy was then held responsible by all in the room for the impact of her harm, and there was no acknowledgment of the sentiments of exclusion that she internalized when she was met with those images. Not valuing the perspective of a person of color is an example of how white supremacy wields power and dismisses non-white sentiments as less-than and antagonistic.

Early in the twentieth century, W. E. B. Du Bois argued that Black people live a double consciousness, one through their own lens and the other through the interpretations of white society.[4] While things have changed in the twenty-first century, this double consciousness is still present in how people of color look into, try to fit into, and rebel against white culture. If we want to strengthen the system of advantage based on race, we can simply ignore that a culture of white supremacy exists and call this viewpoint "extremist." If we wrestle with and begin to accept the idea that whiteness is the dominant culture, we will then better understand what needs to change in our schools.

White Privilege

As people in positions of power, educators need to ask: What is our responsibility in dismantling a system that advantages one race over others? To do this kind of work, we need to check our privileges and biases. *Privilege* is having access to power based on certain advantages.[5] We all have privilege, whether based on our race, gender, class, ability, language, religion, or other element of our identity. Recognizing these privileges and the advantages and powers they offer you in certain situations and systems will help you understand the depth of the work ahead.

For example, as an able-bodied, cisgender straight man, who is a US citizen, Henry holds a number of privileges. Kathy is also an able-bodied, cisgender, straight US citizen. Although Kathy shares many of the same privileges as Henry, Henry's gender often grants him privileges that Kathy does not benefit from. It is important that Henry recognizes this distinction and the advantages it gives him in

---

4 W. E. B. Du Bois, *The Souls of Black Folk* (New Haven, CT: Yale University Press, 2015).

5 Frances E. Kendall, *Understanding White Privilege: Creating Pathways to Authentic Relationships across Race* (New York: Routledge, 2012).

particular contexts. We are not asking you to be ashamed or guilty of your privileges, but to do the work of antiracism, it is essential we acknowledge them so that we can support people who do not have the same advantages.

There are many examples of exercises that help one examine their own privilege, which eventually can be used to engage your staff in the same examination. These exercises can be helpful not only for delineating all the possible areas of privilege, they can also help people see where they don't have privilege—allowing them to reflect on how this feels for them, and how others might also feel about their own lack of privilege in areas such as race, class, gender, sexuality, ability, education, citizenship, religious belief, body size, and more.

Below is an example of an activity you can use with a group that will highlight the awareness and perceived experiences of one's prevalent identities:

Social Identity Activity

Materials: Printed on a piece of paper or shared on a large screen, list various social identities that one may hold. Some examples include:

- Age
- Body size/type
- Country of origin/citizenship
- (Dis)ability
- Ethnicity
- Gender
- Health
- Race
- Religion/faith
- Sexual orientation

- Social class
- Tribal or Indigenous affiliation
- Other (always offer this option in order to avoid excluding one's identity)

Activity:

1. Ask those in the room to quietly choose the identity they are most conscious of at most times (despite the urge to choose more than one, try to encourage them to choose the most prevalent). They do not need to share with others.

2. Once they have chosen, ask them to quietly answer the following questions:

    a. Have you ever felt discriminated against or marginalized because of this identity?
    b. Have you ever felt powerless because of this identity?
    c. Have you ever had someone dismiss your experience or feelings of discrimination, marginalization, or powerlessness regarding this identity?

3. Allow participants to process their responses before asking them (while still keeping their answers to themselves): Is it possible that you have ever (intentionally or unintentionally) caused someone else to feel that way?

Discussion: Ask if anyone is willing to share what these experiences were like for them.

A theme that commonly arises during this activity is that participants generally choose an identity they are conscious of because it does not fall within the dominant culture of where they work or reside. Such identities are often associated with experiences of marginalization. For example, women often choose gender, BIPOC often choose race, ethnicity, or country of origin, members of the LGBTQ+ community often choose sexual orientation, and so on. In contrast, very rarely do men have a broad consciousness of their gender, or white people of their race, nor heterosexuals of their sexual orientation, as these identities are often part of a broader dominant and normalized culture. This can prompt a deeper conversation about privilege and how easy it is to dismiss someone's identity as significant to them if you don't share their experience. By having participants look inward and highlight an identity they are consistently conscious of and that may have led to experiences of marginalization, you will help them make connections that heighten empathy and understanding of what identity means to each person and how privilege is often associated with dominant culture identities.

As a new principal, Henry was taught by students and teachers in the Gender-Sexuality Alliance (GSA) that as a cisgender man, he can use his privilege to support transitioning and questioning people by listing his pronouns. Since that time, he has listed his pronouns next to his signature, whether on social media or email. Just as cisgender men and women can support transitioning and questioning people, so, too, can white people use their white privilege to support people of color and fight racism. When we ignore our privilege, we work to support systems of oppression. In *So You Want to Talk about Race,* author Ijeoma Oluo describes how she writes down all of her privileges every year to affirm her recommitment to social justice.[6] Unless we reflect on ourselves, we are hurting the antiracist movement. As antiracist educators, we need to continually reevaluate, adjust, and change our practices based on the needs of individual students.

When one tries to be colorblind, they ignore that white people belong to a race of people with a culture. Through this ignorance, whiteness is viewed as the standard by which all other cultures are judged, with the cultures of people of color seen either as subnorm or as distinct cultural artifacts. This is evident in most school curriculum, which is told through the narratives of white authors, scientists,

---

6 Ijeoma Oluo, *So You Want to Talk about Race* (New York: Seal Press, 2018).

historians, musicians, and others, and only includes the histories and achievements of people of color when they are exceptional. Another way this is evident is when grocery stores are stocked with foods that are traditional within white culture, while the traditional foods of other peoples are placed in the "ethnic" food aisle. If we stand behind the belief that recognizing white privilege is integral to the anti-bias work of white educators, we must offer a broader recognition of the ways in which white standards show up in our everyday lives and our institutional norms.

Learning about Yourself and the Unintended Impact of Racism

One of the best places to start to learn about racism is by focusing on learning about yourself. How do you experience race and racism? What do you know about your own understanding of your racial background and how that common heritage fits within the structures of racism? What do you know and understand about other racial groups? What biases have you developed about those groups? This focus on learning about your own racial identity development and implicit bias allows you to become more aware of your weak spots and where your own growth must be focused.

Racial Identity Development

One of the most critical areas for one to reflect on in this journey is our racial identity. Racial identity is defined as "the meaning each of us has constructed or is constructing about what it means to be a White person or a person of color in a race-conscious society."[7] From a very early age, we are required to self-select and report our identified racial group into almost every system, e.g., education, health care, employment, etc.

---

7 Beverly Daniel Tatum, *Why Are All the Black Kids Sitting Together in the Cafeteria?: And Other Conversations about Race*, 20th anniversary ed. (New York: Basic Books, 2017).

While we rarely speak about how this identification is embedded in how we learn and how it reaffirms one race as superior and others as inferior, the underlying messages are constantly reinforced and involuntarily become a part of our subconscious.

We have found this to be particularly challenging for white people, and some readers may even find it hard to read language that describes white people as one culture. But if we are to understand race in the United States and work to dismantle the system of advantage, we have to understand that whiteness *is* a culture, and it is the culture that we see as the norm in our society. As Beverly Daniel Tatum writes, "In a race-conscious society, the development of a positive sense of racial/ethnic identity, not based on assumed superiority or inferiority, is an important task for both White people and people of color. The development of this positive identity is a lifelong process that often requires unlearning the misinformation and stereotypes we have internalized not only about others, but also about ourselves."[8] Therefore, as with any racial group, dismantling racism requires white people to commit to learning about their racial identity and ultimately embrace the idea that a "white culture" exists, and it is associated with messages of dominance and superiority.

Think back on your early years and recall one of the first moments you became aware of race or racism. It may have been an experience on the playground in elementary school, something you overheard an adult say, or maybe a scene in a TV show or movie that stuck with you. Despite anyone's will to be colorblind, these moments exist for all of us. Underlying messages about race—not explicit or said aloud—imply that one race is standard and others different; one race is powerful and others inferior; one race is safe and others dangerous. As early as four or five years old, white children subconsciously internalize that they are "lucky" to be white and, without the proper language or tools

---

8 Beverly Daniel Tatum, "Understanding Racial Identity: An Interview with Beverly Daniel Tatum," interview by Parents League of New York, June 10, 2020, parentsleague.org/blog/understanding-racial-identity-interview-beverly-daniel-tatum.

to understand it, this sentiment becomes a part of how they perceive themselves in relation to others.

Racial identity development charts can be found online and summarize several frameworks that have been created to describe these stages for different identity groups and to conceptualize the basic progressions an individual goes through when defining their racial identity. It is important to recognize that these stages are neither linear nor static—people might revisit different stages at different points in their lives or never experience some stages. These charts are intended for self-assessment, not judgment, to better understand that all people have a racial identity that is in some way influenced by power and privilege. These are great documents to use to reflect on the stage you are at and on what it would take to continue to grow.[9]

This learning is critical to become an antiracist and challenges even the most well-intentioned person to consider how their beliefs ultimately result in behaviors and practices that reinforce white students' privilege and opportunity, while causing harm to nonwhite students. This is where the foundation of antiracist work begins: with the acknowledgement and acceptance that societal structures and messages perpetuate our belief systems about race and determine notions of deservedness and fairness.

In workshops, we ask people to remember their first life experience involving race. Often this exercise leads people to tell stories about either an incident that happened to them, an incident they observed, or an incident in which they did something to someone else. When we lead this exercise, we tend to see people of color sharing stories in which something happened to them or they observed something. White people tend to share stories about when they did something to someone else or observed something happen to someone else. Another difference is that people of color tend to tell stories of things that happened when they were young whereas white respondents often tell stories about when they were adolescents or even adults. This

---

9 You can find a chart we use with staff at HenryJTurner.com/ChangeTheNarrative.

exercise helps people understand that people of color are regularly reminded of their race, whereas white people have the privilege to not think about their race. This is true in the same way that cisgender men do not have to think about their gender, heterosexuals do not need to think about their sexuality, etc. When it comes to race, whiteness is the dominant culture.

Many of the choices we make as educators and school leaders are driven by the value-based beliefs and messages we internalized throughout our own educational journey. The rules and structures we perpetuate with good intentions can and do have harmful impacts on our students and colleagues. It is our responsibility to spend time in exploration and reflection. While they may be uncomfortable, these are conversations you will need to keep revisiting with yourself as you prepare to work with your staff on their own racial identity development. We will provide more information on how to engage staff in later chapters.

Conclusion

The information in this chapter is meant to serve as a starting point in your committed journey to becoming an antiracist leader. Before you are able to engage your staff and school community, you must do this work to understand the historical and current structures and implications of racism in the context of our educational systems and the experiences of members of marginalized groups within your school community. You will be asked to reflect on your own values and biases and will be pushed to deconstruct much of what you've been taught about norms and standards that default to whiteness. It will require perseverance, vulnerability, and humility to challenge any impulses to be defensive or overwhelmed by the enormity of the task at hand.

To achieve transformational change, you will also need to commit to the responsibility of creating and supporting learning opportunities for your staff, students, and parent community. The antiracist work needed to dismantle racist ideas and racist policies must be done every moment and every day in our schools. When this work is ignored or when we do not utilize an antiracist mindset the consequences will manifest. When we speak with students who have found themselves in trouble at school, we speak about the decision tree—every decision we make leads to another set of options. When we look back, we realize that we find ourselves in situations not because of one decision but because of many decisions—we find ourselves stuck in the tree. Racism works in much the same way. Racism is not a manifestation of one decision, but of many decisions. When we ignore antiracism in our decision-making, we find ourselves stuck strengthening racism.

KEY IDEAS

- A committed antiracist leader begins with the acknowledgment and acceptance that institutional racism in our educational systems makes this work essential.
- The journey requires a commitment to a lifelong learning process of self-reflection on values and actions that contribute to upholding racist structures.
- An antiracist leader creates learning opportunities for themselves and their school community, inclusive of ongoing assessment and feedback.

CHANGE THE NARRATIVE

LEARN-Research white privilege and white supremacy culture to identify where it shows up in your school community.

REFLECT-Think about times you may have participated in a system or a practice that maintained a hierarchy based on race. What can you do differently with this new information?

ACT-Invest in and support ongoing learning opportunities for yourself and your staff to better understand racial identity and the experiences of marginalized groups within your school community.

ASSESS-Create systems to consistently assess your growth and invite constructive feedback, e.g., evaluation tools, feedback cycles, self-tests, etc.

CHAPTER 3

REFLECT

When we can sit in the face of insanity or dislikes and be free from the need to make it different, then we are free.

—NELSON MANDELA

Alongside any process of learning, reflection is an important, ongoing practice that complements the development of skills and review of their effectiveness. Because the commitment to antiracism requires new learning about oneself, reframing of perspectives, and unlearning of old beliefs, practices, and behaviors, reflection can serve as a powerful tool to pause and check in on your progress. It is also an opportunity to invite others to support your growth and hold you accountable to goals you have set for yourself as a leader. As we anticipate this work will create some chaos and upheaval, a commitment to reflection will help keep you grounded in the process and center your learning so that it is objective and purposeful.

This chapter will help you learn to use reflection to develop your strategic thinking on your antiracist journey and to be intentional about structuring time and processes that expand your capacity to overcome discomfort, accept challenges, and push past the moments where it may be easier to default to old behaviors. We will further explore the importance of being reflective and will share strategies to help you self-reflect and prepare for the next step—action. We cannot overlook the significance of reflection as a tool that will serve you in moments of contradiction, confusion, or exhaustion. The process of reflection allows us to develop both strategy and assurance that our work is indeed antiracist. It's worth noting that we use our practice in yoga and meditation to help inform our work in this chapter.

When using a mindful practice in your antiracist work, you can become more aware of:

- What the real issues bubbling up are.
- Your emotions during this moment.
- Where your comfort zone lies and how to step out of it.
- Commitment to your personal growth as an antiracist.
- A racist idea or structure and how to shift your mindset about it.
- Your previously held racist ideas that require unlearning.

Why Reflection Is Important

We live in a society full of tension and complexity, and in our daily lives, we develop our own patterns and behaviors for how we respond to these complexities. Some of these patterns of response have adjusted over time as we have collected more information about ourselves and our surroundings, but some patterns show up as a default, with limited process or reasoning. As a leader, this can be an asset or necessary skill when a split-second decision must be made, but rarely do we pause, return to, and reflect on the choices, behaviors, and patterns that show up as a part of our decision-making or default thinking.

It may sound idealistic and romanticized, but when we simplify the narratives of our experiences or revert to what feels comfortable, we miss opportunities to discover the joy of embracing complexity and the growth that comes from the intentional reflection of who we are and how we show up in moments of complexity or discomfort. "Reflection gives the brain an opportunity to pause amidst the chaos, untangle and sort through observations and experiences, consider multiple possible interpretations, and create meaning. This meaning becomes learning, which can then inform future mindsets and actions."[1] As an antiracist leader, the complexity of the work will routinely present itself as you commit to changing patterns, practices, and behaviors that marginalize and misrepresent particular members of your community. Thoughtful reflection on these practices and your role in supporting or partici-pating in what has been harmful to others may not feel good in the moment, but pausing to listen, learn, and assess will help guide your vision to be more inclusive, productive, and intentional. It can also help ensure that people of color are supported as leaders in your school and that co-conspirators will take action when there are attempts to silence their voices.

While we've likely heard the term *ally* used in this work, we high-light the term *co-conspirator* here because it may be unclear what the difference is between them. Educator and coach Andrew Greenia says that "white people who are striving to be co-conspirators in racial jus-tice work must not only be allies who recognize the impact of racism on people of color, but also active agents of change that realize their own stake in eradicating white supremacy."[2]

Reflection must be a key part of your beginning work, and a con-siderable amount of time should be spent here—despite a desire and pressure to jump into action. When we rush our work and go from learning to action, we often miss the complexities and will likely mis-step. This is true in our day-to-day actions, as well as when we are lead-ing policy and cultural change. Only through reflection do we better understand the tension and contradictions of racism as we endeavor to become antiracists.

---

1   Jennifer Porter, "Why You Should Make Time for Self-Reflection (Even If You Hate Doing It)," *Harvard Business Review*, March 21, 2017, hbr.org/2017/03/why-you-should-make-time-for -self-reflection-even-if-you-hate-doing-it.

2   Andrew Greenia, "The Role of White Co-Conspirators in Dismantling Systemic Racism," Embracing Equity, November 2, 2018, embracingequity.org/blog/2018/11/2/let-us-work -together-the-role-of-white-co-conspirators-in-dismantling-systemic-racism.

Complexity and Tension

When this work is introduced, we have often heard inquisitive learners wonder about the complexity of our racist structures and how to dismantle them. For example, white educators often voice the struggle they encounter when they want to be supportive of colleagues of color but are unclear how to do so. They may perceive messages about how to support and practice allyship in the moment as conflicting. For example, they may be told to amplify the voices of people of color when other colleagues speak over them or take credit for an idea they've introduced—two actions that regularly happen. In response, white educators and colleagues take this as a prompt and do as requested, by interrupting and explaining that the colleague of color has been trying to speak or calling out the person who is taking credit. Another perspective requests that white educators and colleagues take a back seat and let people of color take the lead. Both requests are applicable depending on the moment. At the same time, these same actions could be unwelcome and inappropriate in other situations. Therefore, it is possible for actions to be marginalizing one moment and antiracist the next.

When white educators see these two perspectives in contradiction with each other, they can get frustrated, which may lead them to either inaction—"This work is too hard, I give up"—or inappropriate action, such as defaulting to the easy road—"I'm just going to sit quietly anytime a person of color speaks." While these perspectives do seem to be in contradiction, the reality is that both can be true—white colleagues should help to amplify the voices of colleagues of color and should also sit back to allow colleagues of color to speak for themselves. This is a tension that exists for antiracists, and we must constantly be working on both sides of the rope. This work requires you to see us as individuals and to read situations.

It is also worth noting that more complexity and more tension emerges after we become more aware of race and racism, which is a demonstration of learning. It is because of this complexity that our actions must be thoughtful, culturally appropriate, and responsive to the moment. Only reflection can help us learn this.

Finding the Discomfort

In institutions deeply embedded in white dominance, it is common practice to avoid discomfort and simplify the narrative. This practice is dominated by a desire to center comfort for those who are within the majority—white people—while leaving out the experiences and needs of those who are less represented or marginalized—people of color. One of the reasons it is critical to sit in reflection is because learning about race and racism can hit us hard with feelings of discomfort. For example, we may get defensive when a colleague gives us negative feedback based on a comment we made or an action we took. We may discard their feedback and move forward, particularly if we feel that our action was focused on equity. In our experience, this reflection step may be the one most often missed in our learning development. For many of us, we love to learn, but we don't like to be wrong.

Bypassing reflection can be a defensive strategy that prevents one from sitting with discomfort. Antiracism is about challenging the pre-conceived racist ideas we have always considered the norm. Therefore, reflection in this work requires us to sit with our discomfort, which can take time to fully process. As Black school leaders, we have had to give feedback around race to white colleagues that has left them feeling unsettled. When an action or comment they make is offensive and they are called on it, their initial reaction is to shut down, particularly in the context of a meeting or other public setting. But if we are to learn more, we have to find a way to sit with that discomfort.

Antiracist reflection is allowing ourselves to hear the comment a person of color is making, sit with it, and process its validity. This kind of reflection demonstrates to the other person that they are being listened to, that their voice is valued, and that there is a commitment to understanding for the purpose of action. Receiving feedback can be challenging for many of us and may elicit feelings of shame or embarrassment, particularly when given in the presence of observers. Our own unconscious biases can also cause us to discredit feedback from a person of color due to our own socially constructed ideas of authority and power. In order to minimize these reactions, which are ultimately barriers to moving the work forward, it is important to create norms about the purpose of feedback and to ground it in our shared learning. If we default to resistance, rather than pause for reflection, we miss the opportunity to learn, grow, and take action. This work takes time and practice, and particularly for leaders, must be revisited often.

One time during Henry's yoga practice, the instructor said, "Move around and look for the uncomfortable spots in the pose. Stay and breathe into that uncomfortable spot just like an uncomfortable conversation." The teacher remarked that if you want to get out of this discomfort, that's when you know you need the pose the most. The same is true in this work; we need to find that discomfort to determine the direction of our work.

Questions for Critical Reflection

Critical reflection is a protocol for deep self-study. You can use it to help you reflect on big-picture items, such as your progress in this work, or specific areas, such as a goal or incident.

- What's the current reality?
- Why did it happen?
- What does it mean?
- What can I do next?
- Whom should I include in next steps?

Thoughtful Responses Require Thought

As educators, we are constantly making decisions in a fast-paced environment, so it is understandable that we miss the critical step of reflection. Discussing the importance of self-reflection in the *Harvard Business Review*, executive leadership coach Jennifer Porter highlights why leaders don't like process: "Reflection requires leaders to do a number of things they typically don't like to do: slow down, adopt a mindset of not knowing and curiosity, tolerate messiness and inefficiency, and take personal responsibility."[3] If we view our work around racism in this same manner, we neglect those we hurt and gain little understanding of the cause of success when we act.

Finding urgency in getting started in this work is different than expecting our actions to lead to an immediate outcome. As described in chapter 1, the faster we respond, the more apt our internal biases are to influence our thinking. Furthermore, we are more likely to take on practices that support our preconceived ideas. This is how many of our practices, even when the intention is to dismantle racism, end up creating more inequity. All of this can set us back even further in our work. Reflective practice allows us to be more efficient than when we take an urgency mindset.

Persistence and Resilience

Two important aspects of antiracism are demonstrating persistence in this work and developing the resilience to continue despite pushback. Resistance to racism comes with many failures, criticisms, and setbacks. When looking at antiracist heroes of the past, their resilience—the ability to absorb, adapt, and transform in response to a shock or long-term stressor—show up consistently. What made historic figures like Nat Turner lead a slave rebellion? Ida B. Wells fight the violence of lynching? Cesar Chavez take on the large agricultural industry? John

---

3 Porter, "Self-Reflection."

Lewis stand in the face of the Alabama police, or Ruth Bader Ginsburg write dissenting opinion after dissenting opinion? A common theme for all of them was their persistence to think big to overcome this system of oppression and inequity and their resilience to weather loss. The same is true in leadership in schools. We should use these models to inspire us to continue in our work.

Antiracist work is fatiguing, so even when we commit to it, we are likely to burn out when we attempt to act with blunt force instead of thoughtful strategy. Reflection is the critical step that allows us to persevere and survive in this work, as well as find actions of success. The point is that if we truly commit to changing the narrative, then we need to commit to this step, slow down, find meaning in what we are learning, and make the connections we need to be able to grow our practice.

Often we suppress emotions of discomfort, sadness, or disappointment when in a process of change—internally or externally—but suppressing feelings can manifest in different ways and, in this work, lead to burnout. Reflection in the forms of meditation, prayer, journaling, and other spiritual practices can be powerful in processing emotions in transformative ways and in building resiliency. Our history shows us that many acts of resilience by Black people in the United States were fortified by prayer and religion. Social justice movements and spiritual practices often go hand in hand to balance the physical labor of action and emotional labor of contemplation, reinforcing persistence, and resiliency to the cause.

Radical Self-Care

When we commit to this tireless work, our commitment to take care of ourselves is just as critical. Finding moments to step away from the work is essential in our self-preservation. Poet Audre Lorde's celebrated declaration that "Caring for myself is not self-indulgence, it is self-preservation, and that is an act of political warfare" describes radical self-care as necessary and unapologetic.[4] Self-care can look like spending time with family and friends, going for a walk, exercising, or meditating, but it can also look like simply turning off—whether taking a nap, shutting off your phone, or leaving email responses until the morning. These types of activities allow us to distance ourselves from the daily grind of this work and give us the space to pause and reflect. When we practice self-care, we are also pushing against the structures of racial oppression that are determined to grind us up.

Racism is always present, even when prioritizing time to take care of ourselves. We must be mindful of the disparities in accessibility, resources, and even time for self-care in communities of color and low-income communities. Nevertheless, when we take time for ourselves, we can do it in a manner that honors the work we are doing. Self-care is about giving ourselves the space we need to reflect on our work. We can accomplish this by being antiracist, as well.

Conclusion

Reflection is a critical step in the cycle of becoming an antiracist leader and educator. It pushes us to pause and consider the ways we are contributing to the problem, but also opens us up to invite in new voices, consider new approaches, and learn about how we show up in this work. It cannot be overlooked as a valuable component of antiracist work and will require us to spend a significant amount of time encouraging a culture of reflection—for ourselves and our colleagues. Rather than jumping into action, spend time listening, processing, and trying new methods to reflect on what feels challenging. Reflection is an opportunity to transform ourselves as antiracist practitioners. Be open to the possibility that reflection doesn't have a timeline: it is messy, and it requires regular practice. There is no peak with antiracist practice. We continue to grow in this work. Know that you are going to have victories and failures as you open yourself to transformation.

---

4 Audre Lorde, *A Burst of Light: Essays* (Ithaca, NY: Firebrand Books, 1988).

KEY IDEAS

- Reflection is a critical step in the cycle of becoming an antiracist educator. When this step is overlooked, we are more apt to miss something, which can result in actions that are either ineffective or reinforce a racist structure. When we don't reflect, we miss the opportunity to learn.
- Reflection allows us to step away from the work to recharge and find space. Utilize reflection as an opportunity to build resilience and perseverance in this work.
- Mindfulness practices encourage us to be present and to recognize what may be lying underneath internal and external conflict. This conflict is always present in our work as antiracist educators.
- There are many mindful practices, such as journaling, meditation, exercise, walking, and prayer. These practices allow us to uncover and process our emotions—both positive and negative.

CHANGE THE NARRATIVE

LEARN-Watch a video of Angela Davis explaining radical self-care.[5]

REFLECT-Consider your values, beliefs, and challenges as an antiracist leader. How can a mindfulness practice positively impact your role as a leader in managing crises, chaos, and conflict?

ACT-Research different reflection and mindfulness practices and choose one that fits your needs and style. Then begin your practice.

ASSESS-Use a journal to write down your process and goals, and revisit your growth and progress.

---

5 "Radical Self Care: Angela Davis," AFROPUNK, video 4:27, December 17, 2018, youtu.be/ Q1cHoL4vaBs.

CHAPTER 4

ACT

Action is the only remedy to indifference: the most insidious danger of all.

—ELIE WIESEL

New leaders are vulnerable to making big mistakes, because they are unfamiliar with the school culture and do not yet feel adept in their job. An entry plan is a great strategy to help leaders feel more in control. When we began our roles, we used Barry Jentz's book *Entry* to guide us through the all-important first year.[1] As new administrators, this book helped us make some sense of what we were supposed to do at work during a time when we knew very little. It offers a step-by-step process for learning about your organization and role, helping to guide leaders through a time when, despite knowing very little about the role and (possibly) the school, people expect and need them to make decisions. It can help you craft your opening letter, design entry surveys for your school community, create focus groups, and incorporate other strategies so you can learn about the organization. This support is essential because when we have the least experience, we have the greatest potential to make big mistakes.

When Henry accepted the position of principal at Newton North High School, he was excited to work in a school district he had worked

---

1 Barry C. Jentz, *Entry: The Hiring, Start-up, and Supervision of Administrators* (New York: McGraw-Hill, 1982).

in before. He knew this job would be complicated and challenging but rewarding at the same time. In the few months between accepting and starting his dream job, Henry created an entry plan. This plan included surveying the community, asking questions to educators, parents, and students, and learning about the strengths and needs of the school. He figured this would be the focus of his first fall and most likely the winter, as well. He was determined to slow himself down and to understand the culture.

When he began that July, he woke up every morning feeling he needed to pinch himself, he felt so lucky. Having been a principal before, he planned to start slow and build relationships. He knew there was a lot of work to do, particularly given the toxicity of the upcoming 2016 US presidential election between Donald Trump and Hillary Clinton at the time, which was a very divisive election that engaged racist tropes and anti-immigrant sentiment, and threatened to make racist speech acceptable in polite company again. As the campaigning became even more inflammatory in the fall, the beginning of the school year for Henry's first year would be even more complicated.

On September 27, Henry's plan for a slow entry was upended. Only three weeks into the school year, a group of students drove around the front half-circle driveway of Newton North High School— "Tiger Drive"—several times, honking the car horn and waving the Confederate flag. As they were doing this, another student caught the spectacle on video and posted it to social media. The video went viral.

Knowing barely anyone in the building, Henry met with his administration team that afternoon for his first emergency meeting. Aware that they were in a crisis, he and the deans began investigating the incident. The investigation, however, was outpaced by the video being shared on social media and the reactions it received. Then the media picked up the story and called Henry, looking for a response. The superintendent reached out to offer support, knowing that this would be the first crisis that he would be dealing with as a new principal, and emails and phone calls from concerned parents flooded in.

Henry met with the students of the combined junior and senior elective course Leadership in a Diverse Society. This course had been created by an earlier principal in the 1990s, when racial tension at the school was high. The goal is to bring together leaders who represent the school's diversity to discuss issues surrounding racism, sexism, homophobia, and other forms of hate.

Because he was new to the school, Henry could not begin to understand the range of emotions these students were feeling. They expressed that they were already angry from recent racist and antisemitic graffiti that had appeared in the school the previous the spring. However, students of color also expressed their hurt and pain from twelve to thirteen years of schooling within a racist society, in which they and their friends experienced racist acts and micro- and macroaggressions from classmates and adults. These students felt disconnected in an environment that was meant to help them thrive. The message was: They were going to protest with or without the administration's support.

By September 28, it was increasingly clear students wanted a protest and they wanted to do it at school. Announcements on social media called for protests at Newton North, inviting nonstudents to participate, as well. Local civil rights organizations shared the message with their followers on social media. With this also came rumors of white supremacist groups threatening to protest at the football game and civil rights groups planning to form a counterprotest. Henry felt the pressure for this to go well, but the situation was dependent on the decisions of the students. But as the day went on, Henry was still not able to work out a plan with them. When he met with some of the student leaders, they were insistent on holding a walkout at school. He tried to persuade them that having an event inside the building was safer. Later that day, he sent the faculty an email explaining the possible events that could happen: student protest, walkout, march, outsiders joining, etc.

Still in his office at 10:00 p.m., Henry was finishing up a letter to the staff when he received an email from the student leaders asking if he was able to speak with them via Google Meet. He jumped on his computer. During the conversation, they expressed their desires. Henry and the student leaders all agreed they wanted students' voices to be heard. The students wanted to make a difference, and Henry wanted to support them and keep everyone safe. With this understanding, they began negotiating the terms of a student protest:

- A protest at school in the building at the end of the day
- Student speakers
- Stay on campus
- Students and staff only

As he headed home late that night, he was extremely uneasy about whether this event would work. He knew he was putting his dream job on the line, but what he did not know was that he and the students were taking the first steps to establishing ground rules for what student activism could look like in their school.

The next morning, Henry and the vice principal joined the student organizers, which included students from Leadership in a Diverse Society. The meeting was emotional. Students of color expressed anger. They wanted to make it clear that they felt the school did not care about or support them. They refused to accept the limited agreement that Henry and the student leaders had negotiated the previous evening. Henry explained why he could not support their walkout or their wish for outsiders to join, and that he was worried about their safety.

Later in the morning, one of the student leaders asked to speak with Henry, and they both expressed hope that their talk would be successful. Ultimately, they came to an agreement to allow a protest with student speakers in the cafeteria.

With over five hundred students and staff in attendance, the event lasted about forty-five minutes and included a range of speakers. Expressing their frustration, the students shared examples of the racism they would experience daily, from both students and staff, and spoke about the lack of connection they felt with the school. They called for change. At the end of the protest, Henry took the microphone and expressed his support for the movement and his pride that their school had been able to host such an event. The pride of the student organizers was clear, too. They knew they were making a difference in their school.

For a school leader, it can often feel like the work is full of crises that require immediate action. During this crisis, it was clear that decisions needed to be made quickly and there was immense pressure to make the "right" decision. As leaders, we need to learn how to make decisions in a crisis, but we also need to know when we can be more deliberate in our decision-making so that we don't make every incident a crisis. While our roles certainly require quick decisions to mitigate crises and fast-paced events, most of our actions can be more thoughtful and less immediate. We have learned that the most powerful answer to urgent questions is "I don't know, and I'll get back to you." When we slow down, we are able to be more strategic in our thinking and more deliberate in the steps we take, which helps us recognize our biases and stay focused on our mission of social justice leadership.

This chapter will discuss how we can act as social justice leaders, both in crises that require quick action and in the more common moments when we can use strategic action to make sustainable change to dismantle racism. We will wrap up by discussing the important steps we should take in communication. Even though some of these actions move more swiftly than others, learning and reflection are always important steps to take.

Responding to a Crisis

A few years back, Newton North had a series of incidents in which students made racist posts on social media. As is the nature of social media, information about these posts spread quickly and widely, necessitating fast action to uncover what happened, who did it, and how to respond. In the past when an incident like this would occur, the administration was inclined to default to protecting student privacy and, as a result, not identify the offender. However, prioritizing the offender's privacy leaves the community, and particularly people of color, hurt and unsettled.

During this investigation, Henry's team was able to identify the creators of the posts and respond to support the victims and address the incidents. They followed the harassment and discrimination policy protocols and documented the incident and were able to use restorative practices to help heal the situation. The school administrators felt satisfied knowing the process had worked and that they were able to provide closure for students. They felt they had created a textbook example of how to handle these incidents.

When the administrators met with a group of students of color about the response, however, they discovered the students were mad: rightfully mad that incidents like these were continuing to happen in their school, but also mad at the school's response. "Yes, you handled this," they said, "but we don't think you care that it happened." The administrators were stunned. They thought they had done everything correctly, and they *were* upset this had happened. But during the conversation, the students called the administrators out on something—they hadn't demonstrated to the community how they felt about what was happening in their school.

The message learned from this incident is that we can check all the boxes in addressing a hate incident in our school, but if we become too formulaic, we lose the personal side of the issue. And that is the problem with urgent action: we can become too robotic. In chapter 3, we wrote that the problem with urgent action is that it makes it difficult to be inclusive. The lesson here for the administrators was to move even more deliberately to allow themselves time to demonstrate an empathetic acknowledgment and to share their own pain. This incident showed them that as school leaders, they need to make clear that hate incidents are an attack on the entire community and that they, too, are part of the community. Then the focus can turn to the investigation and finding a resolution.

As administrators, we are pressed for time in addressing incidents. The steps that we offer in this section will help you make sure that your response is both timely and inclusive. These steps include:

- Empathetic acknowledgment
- Investigation
- Communicating the process
- Resolving the situation
- Communicating the resolution

Empathetic Acknowledgment

When we learn of racist incidents and emotions are running high, we need to check ourselves on how we are personally feeling. Remember that the antiracist leader mindset includes the personal lens, therefore these events may be triggering in many ways for us. Maybe we were a victim of a racist attack? Maybe we were the aggressor in a racist attack as a child? Maybe we have been called to task because we made a mistake during an investigation? Whatever the issue, we need to do a self-awareness check, knowing that we will be spending time supporting others.

Leading an investigation as a school administrator is complex and challenging. Some of our students carry personal traumas that we may or may not be aware of, yet weigh heavily on us directly and indirectly. Many students walk through school doors with mental health issues, personal and familial experiences of domestic or substance abuse, grief, and financial constraints due to poverty—just to name a few. Being exposed to these traumas on a frequent basis can lead to feelings of overwhelm and hopelessness. As a survival tactic, we may begin to emotionally detach ourselves in order to manage an investigation process and other procedures. While this is understandable, when we become detached from this work, we run the risk of creating too much distance from student experiences, and seeming unapproachable and unempathetic. Have you ever been busy dealing with three different complex cases and you are walking down the hallway with your brain running at 100 miles an hour, when a student approaches you to ask a simple yet all too familiar question, "Can you help me find my phone?" How do you handle this scenario? Do you pause to help them? Do you tell them to find someone else? Does it depend on who the student is? Moments like these can inform us how well we are staying connected with our students and with our ability to show empathy.

When we are distant and detached, our implicit bias is bound to influence our decision-making. Considering the challenges of our work, how do we show up for students so that we demonstrate empathy, regardless of what their crisis is or who they are? Furthermore, how do we show up for them when they are grieving a racist incident?

We can show empathy by expressing our own anger and frustration along with the community, we can help the community begin to heal. In *Dare to Lead,* Brené Brown describes the difference between sympathy, which states, "I feel bad for you," and empathy, which states, "I feel with you."[2] Sympathy shows our students that they are on their own to grieve in this moment, whereas empathy builds a connection to our students of color that lets them know they are not alone when these incidents happen.

---

2 Brené Brown, *Dare to Lead: Brave Work. Tough Conversations. Whole Hearts.* (New York: Random House, 2018).

Demonstrating Empathy after a Racist Incident

1. Go visit the students who are upset, letting them know that their feelings are valid, and that you will respond to the incident.
2. One way to demonstrate empathy is to say, "You are not alone; this is an attack on your school, as well. We are going to investigate this incident, and we are going to circle back to you to see how you are doing and give you updates on the next steps."
3. Make a plan for checking back in with them.
4. If necessary, reach out to students' counselors, family members, or other trusted adults to help support the student.
5. Reflect on what you learned in this incident from the students before you begin the investigation.

Investigation

Every school and/or district should have standard procedures in place for investigating hate incidents and other forms of discrimination and harassment.[3] Make sure you follow the procedure thoroughly. Update the community on the investigation. A pitfall in this kind of investigation is that we may treat an incident like this as we would a typical name-calling scenario, where we speak with a few possible witnesses or alleged offenders, and if we do not get any leads, we move on. As with any marginalized group, people of color may mistrust the institution and assume that this incident is going to be insufficiently investigated. These aggressions and microaggressions, make small cuts that constantly demoralize people of color, and this is only made worse by our refusal to acknowledge those cuts or to acknowledge the existence of racism. It is important that you thoroughly follow every lead

---

3 School districts should also have a specific discrimination investigation and reporting protocol.

possible, no matter how long it takes. The victims in this incident need to know that you did everything you could to investigate.

Communicating the Process

Hate incidents are attacks on the community and should be treated as such. Deciding when to notify the community is tricky because notifying the community too early can hamper your investigation or risk spreading misinformation, but you also have to make sure your process is transparent and that you are demonstrating your anger on behalf of the community. The timing is really based on your understanding of your community and of the incident. There have been times when our messages to the community came too early and we did not have all the information, or came too late, when rumors were already spreading, or when we got the timing just right. Unfortunately, it is only with experience that you will get a sense of what is right for your community.

Some school leaders have told us that they have been trained not to communicate with the school community about racist messages or graffiti because it leads to copycats. This kind of advice assumes that students do not know about events happening at the school or in the world more broadly, which is increasingly not true in the age of social media. Inaction of this kind also reinforces the notion that we do not care and that we are sweeping these incidents under the rug. Forgoing communication is not okay. This perpetuates the message that racist incidents are the norm and that we don't need to talk about them. These incidents should never feel that way.

We have been involved in investigations where we felt we understood the situation but did not have enough information to move forward with any action. Proactive communication *is* action. Let the community know where you are in the investigation.

Resolving the Situation

Incidents such as this can move in thousands of different directions. You may or may not be able to identify the offender, or it may end up being a "they said, they said" incident. Nonetheless, it is important to move forward. If you identified the offender, provide the appropriate consequence according to your student handbook. (We will spend more time on discipline and restorative practices in chapter 10.) Taking action to respond to the offender according to the guidelines of your school policy is important because it sends a message to the victims that you have taken the incident seriously.

If you are unable to identify the offender, there are still actions you can take. These steps should include checking to make sure all leads were followed and every attempt was made to understand the incident from different perspectives. Bring others into the situation to help provide feedback about other steps that you can take. We have drawn on educators in various roles to ensure a variety of perspectives during investigations, bringing in those who can challenge our process to ensure we have addressed all leads. One note: from Kathy's position as a director for diversity, equity, and inclusion and Henry's as a principal, we can soundly affirm that principals should not pass the responsibility of this investigation on to the DEI director. While the DEI director can be a great source of support, the school building administrators, as antiracist leaders, need to take responsibility for seeing these incidents through.

Communicating the Resolution

Regardless of whether you were able to identify the offender or not, make sure that you communicate the resolution to the community. What actions did you take? What actions do you plan to take to reduce the potential for incidents like this again? Always remember to demonstrate empathy. People of color need to know that their leader is in it with them.

There are many possible scenarios that can arise, whether at school, off campus, or on social media like the incident we discussed earlier. Different forms of crises or incidents will require different kinds of responses. But even if you encounter a situation that doesn't require you to follow all of these steps, it is important to make sure that you check yourself using this list. For example, if you were handling an incident that happened off campus, you may not need to investigate because no school rules have been broken. However, it is very likely students of color will feel harmed and require steps such as empathetic acknowledgement, communicating the process of what the school can and cannot do, providing a resolution, and communicating your response.

Strategic Action: Creating Sustainable Change

After the rally in response to the Confederate flag incident, the students' voices had been heard and the values of the school demonstrated. When Henry woke up the following Monday, he could have easily felt "we solved it" and moved on, getting back to his entry plan. But addressing systemic racism is as much about the work you do when things are quiet as when crises erupt. From what he knew, students' emotions were still raw; students of color made speeches about their school not being a place that was designed to support them. Furthermore, the tensions of the 2016 election were growing along with tensions in the school.

As a first-year principal, Henry did not have the political capital or the knowledge of the school for wholesale change. He needed to find small ways to make an impact. Soon after the rally, he went to Sue, who teaches Design and Visual Communications, a four-year program in the Career Technical Education Department. He asked Sue if the students could create something that would help demonstrate the core values in the school. She brainstormed some ideas for how she could make this project the central focus of the program, but not yet knowing much about the program, Henry thought at best they would put up a few posters. Little did he know what would ensue. Sue's program uses the design thinking process to allow students to create. Over the next several years, students conducted market research, learning about public art, cultural patterns, fundraising, and other elements needed to design and develop a piece of public art that now stands in the center of the main hallway, which the school refers to as "Main Street."

The final image includes rolling hills in the background, with words student researchers gathered from their classmates by asking what comes to mind when they think about the school's core values. A tree representing learning and growth holds photos of different community members on its branches. Three tigers in the image represent the creative student, the competitive student, and the student leader—each with different cultural patterns that represent the diversity of the school.

The project is ongoing. The intention is to eventually make the images 3-D; nevertheless, when the students' poster showed up on Main Street, it was a demonstration of the power of student creation to change the story. Contrary to an image of students waving the Confederate flag, this public artwork showed that our community is strengthened by our differences.

Seven graduating classes collaborated on this project over six years. During this time, students not only developed incredible skills in their area of design, they also helped shift the school culture. Every step of the way, they made an impact. The project helped foster more antiracism in our school in many ways—by being student focused, collaborative, and a tool for communication.

Because racism is so ever present and amorphous, our actions to dismantle it should be strategic. We need to celebrate the small wins while also focusing on moving forward. Whether small or large, our actions should incorporate a plan for execution based on our learning and reflection. The next section will focus on things to keep in mind as we move forward.

Learning Organization

The first course of the principal preparation program Henry teaches is focused on organizational change. The goal of the course is to help aspiring leaders learn how to foster second-order change in their schools. In a nutshell, second-order change is big, culture-shifting, long-lasting change. Toward the middle of the course, students play a board game called Systems Thinking, Systems Changing by the Network Inc. This game is one of the more memorable aspects of the entire program, because students finally connect with what they have learned throughout the earlier half of the course—a big change requires many small steps, thoughtfully done and in a logical process. Similar to the change game, Peter Senge's classic *The Fifth Discipline* describes the five disciplines of a learning organization—personal mastery, mental models, a shared vision, team learning, and systems thinking—and highlights the importance of the fifth discipline, systems thinking. Systems thinking is a holistic approach to studying how all aspects of an organization are interconnected. As systems-thinking expert Russ Ackoff explains, "A system is a whole that cannot be divided into independent parts or subgroups of parts."[4] When we use systems thinking as a lens for change, we are able to develop a strategy that will account for the fact that decisions and actions have an impact on the organization as a whole. Therefore, as antiracist leaders, we need to be mindful that we are not just making change for the sake of change but utilizing a strategy to shift the culture. Systems thinking is strategic thinking.

The reality is that examples of successful antiracist acts are strategic. In chapter 3 we discussed the power of reflection for civil rights leaders. These leaders have also been expert strategic thinkers, for example, in using civil disobedience, linking the importance of reflection with strategic action. Activists employing civil disobedience tactics did not get arrested just for the sake of getting arrested—that would not make the news. They strategically got arrested to illuminate unjust

---

4 Russell L. Ackoff, "Systems Thinking and Thinking Systems," *System Dynamics Review* 10, no. 2–3 (1994): 175–188.

laws. They got arrested en masse to fill jails. They used nonviolence to demonstrate the violence of racism. They used television to capture all of this. Their use of strategic thinking moved public perception, upended racist ideas, and changed racist policies.

Our actions are most effective when they are strategic. Change in any school takes time and requires strategy, and when the focus is on dismantling racism within your school, that change becomes even more complicated. When we utilize the systems-thinking lens, we can see that we are all connected and therefore able to learn with each other. This starts with being selective about what topics to focus on. Trying to change everything at once is bound to fail (remember the diagram of categories for an antiracist culture in chapter 1). However, starting with changes that have the best potential to succeed is an effective strategy because these changes tend to be straightforward and popular with at least some people in the school. For example, having students create a mural around core values is something that almost everyone can get behind. Therefore, initial actions should start small with the intent to scale up.

Scaling up change should be collaborative throughout the school where people are engaging and learning together. Senge described a learning organization where "people continually expand their capacity to create the results they truly desire, where new and expansive patterns of thinking are nurtured, where collective aspiration is set free, and where people are continually learning how to learn together."[5] In dismantling racist policies, as the community sees the success of smaller initiatives, you will be able to gain more buy-in for the more controversial and complicated topics. Learning organizations become more collaborative. While this is time-consuming, it allows for educators to push each other's thinking and build trust. Work on dismantling racism can paralyze people; therefore, this approach allows people to develop more comfort and confidence.

---

5 Peter M. Senge, "The Fifth Discipline," *Measuring Business Excellence* 1, no. 3 (1997): 46–51.

Six years after the Confederate flag incident, we can look back and see the improvement that has occurred, to where racial equity is now a central part of our work. Additionally, the outcomes of this work, such as improved connections with students of color, changes to policies and practices, and more discussion about race and racism, are linked to the work we did with our system. Looking back at the "Main Street Project," it is clear the experience had a profound impact on the students who participated in designing and creating it. But the project also had an impact on the larger organization, leading to other acts of antiracism in the school.

Empowering Others

There was a lot of energy to take action in the aftermath of the Confederate flag incident. Leaders must always consider how to capture this energy. As an antiracist leader, collaboration should be front and center in your work. While there may be temptation to make decisions independently, the more collaborative your decision-making, the better.

In line with the cycle of inquiry of learn-reflect-act-assess, it is important to ensure that others around you are committed to this work as well. Welcoming differences of opinion is critical to mitigating group dynamics such as groupthink. Additionally, if we are not thoughtful about racial group dynamics, we are vulnerable to creating racial inequities within a group. Here are a few things to keep in mind when attempting to address racial inequity in committee work:

- The more central racial identity development is to the school's core work, the more likely interested committee members will have either a solid base in this work already, or at least an interest and awareness.
- Broaden the pool of members in the committee. Sometimes in schools we have folks who regularly volunteer for committees. While there may be many positives to their participation—they

get work done, they are active group members, etc.—their involvement can prevent others from joining.

- Encourage a diverse group. Racial diversity is important in this work. You also want to consider years of experience, subject areas, or grade levels taught.
- White saviors are people who view people of color as victims who need to be saved.[6] They proclaim their commitment to this work, but seek praise over results.

Avoiding these potential pitfalls is important to sustaining the work. At the same time, when racial identity is central to your purpose, maintain a growth mindset, understanding that people will develop and improve. Part of empowering others is addressing those who too often dominate the conversation, as well as encouraging engagement from those who typically do not participate. The more you foster a collaborative environment truly focused on equitable engagement, the more voices you will hear from. A measure of success in empowering others is when more people begin to volunteer for committee work or speak up during meetings. But remember, this work is ongoing.

Develop a Systemic Plan

So far in this section we have focused on fostering a learning organization and empowering others to participate. Once you have addressed these facets of strategic action, the final priority is to develop a systemic plan to dismantle racism and inequity in your school or district. There are many great resources for strategic planning and school improvement that can be helpful in designing a plan for building a

---

6 Think about any movie with a white teacher and Black and brown students. Because they are so passionate about this work, we too often empower them in our schools, and they can fall into this category when they are not reflecting on their own work. Unfortunately, they can uphold a power dynamic that shuns other white educators who are interested in this work and also reinforces racist ideas, such as lower expectations for students of color. One important note is that, in our experience, these people are not self-aware and have never received feedback about the negative impacts of their actions. In fact, they may typically get praised because they are some of the few people highlighting racial inequity. As a committed antiracist leader, providing feedback to help them improve is critical.

more equitable school.[7] When you are focused on fostering a learning organization and empowering others, your process should be more inclusive. But it is important to remember that racism is a complex system. Therefore, keep in mind the following recommendations.

See actions through

Educators are used to ambitious changes falling flat and petering out. Speak with any experienced educator and they will remember being extremely passionate about a change and then seeing it vanish before it took hold. Pragmatically, there are always going to be compromises and tweaks we have to make, but it can be demoralizing when people see the potential without realizing lasting results. Seeing your actions through is critical to building the energy and confidence your community needs to dismantle racism.

Celebrate early wins

One way to build that energy is to celebrate your achievements. Whether it is showing your success on social media or having a faculty or student celebration, help your community get excited about the progress you are making. Creating change in schools is hard work. When we focus on dismantling racism, there will be more frustrations than successes. Don't simply move on when one of those successes comes along. Soak it in with the people you worked with, and party!

Strategic action is long and arduous work, but it is also where we can make the deepest impact in our schools. As you see more success in your school you will feel the culture shifting and the momentum building behind this work. The most gratifying moments are when

7 Here are just some: Rachel E. Curtis and Elizabeth A. City, *Strategy in Action: How School Systems Can Support Powerful Learning and Teaching* (Cambridge, MA: Harvard Education Press, 2009); Jim Knight, *Coaching: Approaches and Perspectives* (Thousand Oaks, CA: Corwin, 2008); Andy Hargreaves and Dean Fink, *Sustainable leadership* (San Francisco: Jossey-Bass, 2006); James P. Spillane, *Distributed leadership* (San Francisco: Jossey-Bass, 2006); Donald J. Peurach et al., "From Mass Schooling to Education Systems: Changing Patterns in the Organization and Management of Instruction." *Review of Research in Education* 43, no. 1 (2019): 32–67.

teachers come to you to share a victory or a realization about the inequity they had been perpetuating and make a commitment to changing their practice.

Leadership can feel very lonely, but celebrating your success with others will help you focus on the benefits of this work. The way to move in this direction is to be strategic and plan for the long term. This is antiracist action.

Conclusion

Antiracism is about the work we do to dismantle racist ideas and policies and therefore requires action. This is clearly the most impactful aspect of the cycle of inquiry. But too often we go straight to this step and neglect the learning and reflection steps in the cycle. It is through those steps that we are able to be deliberate in our actions, regardless of whether that action is responding to a crisis, strategic planning, or working on our communication. Regardless of the action, we need to remember to be collaborative, with the goal of empowering others. Once we carry out our actions, we cannot simply move on and forget about them. Rather, we need to move to the final step of the cycle, which is to assess.

KEY POINTS

- Antiracist action should be deliberate so that it can be inclusive. Therefore, before you act, you need to learn and reflect.
- Even when we are involved in a crisis, we need to be deliberate in our work. We should follow these steps:
  - Empathetic Acknowledgment
  - Investigation
  - Communicating the process
  - Resolving the situation
  - Communicating the resolut

- Most of our actions should fall under strategic action. As a system, consider all of the interconnected parts when making a change:
  - Foster the culture as a learning organization.
  - Empower others to work with you to create change.
  - Develop a systemic plan.
  - See actions through.
  - Celebrate early wins.

CHANGE THE NARRATIVE

LEARN-Communicate with your leadership team or your staff on how you work in a crisis.

REFLECT-Complete a postmortem to discuss what steps were taken and what was missed.

ACT-In collaboration with your team, develop a strategic plan for an antiracist action.

ASSESS-How did you empower others, focus on learning, and communicate this plan?

CHAPTER 5

ASSESS

Measure what you value instead of valuing only what you can measure.

—ANDY HARGREAVES

The earlier chapters of this book explain the steps necessary to thoughtfully take action as an antiracist leader, which include learning, reflection, and then action. We have tried to reiterate throughout these sections the importance of deliberate and thoughtful steps through the cycle of inquiry to ensure that your actions effectively dismantle racist ideas and policies and do not create any further harm to traditionally marginalized groups. Antiracist work is hard and time-consuming work where we push to change ideas, systems, and structures that have long existed to reinforce power and privilege for white people. Once we are able to enact a change, that in itself can feel like a victory and a cause for celebration. And while it is always worth celebrating those small wins, it is critical to understand that the work is not done.

Historically, education has been filled with well-intended actions that held the promise of addressing equity but fizzled out, or worse, reinforced existing racist structures and systems. In their book *Tinkering toward Utopia: A Century of Public School Reform*, David Tyack and Larry Cuban demonstrate that promises of policy transformation in schools that end up underdelivering are a reliable fixture in education. "Policy talk about educational reform has been replete with extravagant claims of innovations that flickered and faded. This is a pie-in-the-sky brand of utopianism, and it has often led to disillusionment among teachers and to public cynicism. Exaggeration has pervaded these public rituals of dismay and promise."[1] To ensure that our actions are moving us forward in our work to dismantle racist structures, it is essential that we assess our work, both in small formative assessments, such as check-ins with community members, and in large ways, such as equity audits.

This chapter focuses on assessing our actions to allow social justice leaders to evaluate the progress or lack thereof of antiracist work. Because we make countless decisions every day as educators, it is important that we are strategic about and focused on what we want and need to assess. To conduct a formal and statistically reliable study on every action we make is impractical. Therefore, in this chapter we offer a variety of ways to assess your actions so that you can establish regular informal check-ins and have structures in place for formal assessments, as well. These strategies focus on assessing our personal growth as leaders with an antiracist mindset and on the growth of our school culture in this work. We provide an overview of a number of assessment tools to consider and help you make decisions on when to conduct informal check-ins, when to use a formal tool, and when to ask for outside help to conduct a study.

But the heart of the matter is that it is essential to check our actions, whether small or large. Similar to the reflection step of the cycle of inquiry, assessment forces us to take a step back and understand the impact we are making. It is important to raise up the voices of communities of color during this step to ensure they can provide feedback on the impact of the changes we make. It cannot be said enough that antiracist work must be done every moment of every day. Therefore, it is critical to take a step back and assess our work to ensure that we are

---

1 David B. Tyack and Larry Cuban, *Tinkering toward Utopia: A Century of Public School Reform* (Cambridge, MA: Harvard University Press, 1995).

headed in the direction of more equity, more love, and more success for students of color in our schools.

Evaluating Personal Growth

As school leaders it is essential to regularly step outside our own work to evaluate the effectiveness of our actions and our leadership. Leading with an antiracist lens is no exception. We need to make sure that we are leading effectively and that our work is making a positive impact. Here are some ideas to keep in mind as you focus on assessing your own work.

Self-Evaluation

In her book *So You Want to Talk About Race*, Ijeoma Oluo writes: "I feel very underprivileged as a black, queer woman, and it would be easy to dismiss calls to check my own privilege under the argument that it's really those with a lot of privilege who should be doing the work and I'm too busy fighting racism and sexism to fight the few advantages I do have. But failing to check my own privilege means that my efforts to fight racism and sexism would leave out many of the women and people of color I claim to be fighting for."[2] Taking time to assess the ways in which your privilege and power can show up is an equally important aspect of this work. We have found many educators are interested in taking action to dismantle racism, but are reluctant to evaluate themselves. Activities like the identity activity described in chapter 2 are important to consistently embed in your internal process of assessment. Although many of our privileges are fixed, this strategy pushes us to be cognizant of our role in this system.

Once you have revisited your privilege, begin to assess your personal growth by staying connected to your goal. Write down any personal goals that are connected to antiracist leadership, which can begin with reading books about racial identity or taking advantage

---

2 Ijeoma Oluo, *So You Want to Talk About Race* (New York: Seal Press, 2019).

of educational workshops or training, and eventually shift to broader structural goals, such as creating affinity spaces for staff or offering electives to students that speak to diverse content and cultures. This type of personal assessment builds on your reflective work, but also helps you to evaluate your work.

Goal Setting

When setting goals, it is important to check in on your progress to make sure you are still on track or are addressing barriers that are getting in the way or slowing you down.

Some questions to continuously revisit:
- What action(s) have I taken toward this goal?
- What levers of success have I achieved with this (these) actions(s)?
- Where am I feeling stuck?
- What support do I need to meet this goal?
- How will I know if I'm successful?

You should regularly engage in personal reflection so that you are able to monitor your growth and understanding in this work over time. This type of personal assessment can be part of your regular journaling as described in the reflection section in chapter 3. Some states have begun to include self-evaluation as part of the educator evaluation tool, which could be a useful strategy to encourage educators to reflect on their own growth around racial equity as the school takes on this work.

Feedback Loops for Individual Growth

When Henry was transitioning from one principalship to another, he used the opportunity to get feedback from teachers in the school he was leaving who may not normally have been so honest with him. While he typically conducted anonymous surveys, he used this moment for one-on-one conversations with educators who would give him their unvarnished thoughts. He asked them two questions: "What do I do that's effective?" and "What do I do that's ineffective?" The conversations were invaluable for his own growth, particularly as he was transitioning roles. While conversations like these with people you supervise may be infrequent, it is important to have them with people you trust and who are willing to give you their honest perspective. These kinds of conversions can alert you to areas for growth in this work. They also help get you used to receiving feedback, so that you will be more comfortable getting formal feedback from the larger community.

Formal Feedback

Formal methods of feedback are critical to evaluating your own growth, as well. This is an opportunity to get feedback from either a large group of people, such as the entire staff, or from a more targeted group, such as your BIPOC staff. It is important to be clear about why you are engaged in this formal process and to develop a questionnaire that will get you the kind of answers you are looking for. We have found that requests for feedback can also be opportunities to get input on your progress and to remind the community of your goals.

> Sample language to include in formal feedback to assess progress of a goal:
>
> **Goal:** Learn from and share with each other about the strategies we use to help students develop skills in line with our academic, social, and civic expectations in an antibias environment.
>
> Please rate (_____) on how they accomplished this goal.
>
> Describe one action (if any) that (_____) has taken to demonstrate this goal.
>
> In what way (if any) could (_____) improve upon this goal?

As the busy school year passes, focus on our goals can be lost. But, in addition to giving you clear feedback on your personal growth, this kind of assessment reestablishes your commitment to your goals for both yourself and the school community. Formal methods of feedback can be less frequent than informal feedback loops or even your own self-assessment. Develop a clear strategy to incorporate all three methods of assessment. Receiving a mix of different forms of assessment allows you to get a comprehensive understanding of your progress.

Evaluating School-Based Growth

As school-based leaders, our success is largely based on the growth and improvement of the organization as a whole. We need to ask: How are educators learning and growing together in our school, so that students are learning and growing? So while it is important to monitor our personal growth, it is also critical to understand how our actions work in connection with the overall school growth as we foster an anti-racist culture throughout our schools. This is, ultimately, the purpose of this work: to change the narrative in our schools by helping people jump on board with the work we are leading.

One of the limitations of many books on equity is that they focus only on one's personal growth in this work. While this is important to ignite those who are motivated to do this work, as school leaders, our personal growth is only valuable if we are able to help others to grow, as well. This requires a school culture built upon growing and changing. Therefore, it is critical to use the steps of personal growth—learn, reflect, act, and assess—both as models for school leaders and to help the school culture to grow in this work. Here are some ideas to help you think through assessing the growth of your larger school community.

Staying Connected to Your Goal

In the same fashion as staying connected to your goals for personal growth, it is important for the community to be aware of the goals for the school's growth, as well as where the school stands with its antiracist work. It is important to remember that racism is an old and established system, and dismantling this system will give rise to resistance as well as distractions. Although there will be distractions in your personal growth, they are even more likely when focusing on your community's goals. In the minds of staff, students, and families, there are many competing interests. But dismantling racism requires keeping the focus on race. It is common, for example, for people to focus on other isms as if race could be removed: "Racism isn't the problem, it's socioeconomics" or "Why do we have to focus on race? We should be talking about gender." It is important not to avoid race, which is often a tendency for many people. Race is not in competition with these issues; rather, these issues coexist and reinforce one another. You cannot separate socioeconomics or sexism from race. We cannot talk about poverty without also talking about how marginalized communities are disproportionately affected by it. We cannot talk about gender without recognizing that women of color have a different experience than white women. When people separate these topics from race, the needs of people of color in these categories will often be ignored, which is the history of racism in our country. Help people understand the intersectionality of these issues and that our work is intended to address all of these inequities.

The assessment phase of the learning cycle is a great way to refocus your community on the goals. As you lead community members through an assessment, they will be reminded of the school values and what the school is working toward together. This phase also helps people reflect on their own individual growth, as well as their growth as antiracist educators. With that, your goals should be regularly communicated.

Sharing the goals can be done in both subtle and very straightforward ways. For example, Henry reminds the community of the goal around social justice by including a section of the school's mission statement in his email signature. This small action, in addition to other reminders, helps people in a variety of ways and in a variety of moments to recommit. Here are some examples of strategies to communicate your goal:

- Challenge people in your newsletter to reflect on the school-wide goals.
- Use faculty meetings for a self-assessment in connection to goals.
- Develop a parent-group meeting focused on school goals that incorporates a reading or activity you have done with faculty.
- Conduct a student survey focused on assessing school goals that clearly states the goals.

What you should notice about these strategies is how they are integrated into common activities in the school. Having the community regularly recommit to the goals offers people the opportunity to reflect. This in itself is a nice step toward assessing their, and by extension, the community's progress. But that cannot be it. We also need to ensure we incorporate opportunities for people to offer feedback and share their self-assessment with others.

Feedback Loops for the Community

It is important to establish structures that provide opportunities for feedback for the work of both individuals and the larger community. The feedback should be focused on the goals of the school, and specifically the goals around race, and should be collaborative and growth-based. However, we know that many people are reluctant to receive feedback, and that this is especially true when it is about their work engaging with race and racism. Leaders should therefore ensure all individuals in the school receive feedback on their work around race while also making sure they feel comfortable receiving that feedback without fear of retribution.

The secret sauce to achieving this balance involves several priorities:

- Commitment: People need to trust that this goal of dismantling racism is long lasting and unwavering.
- Modeling: As a leader you are committing to receiving the same kinds of feedback as others.
- Time: People are given the time to go through several iterations of the cycle of inquiry and develop confidence in themselves to receive honest feedback.
- Support: As leaders, we demonstrate a commitment to the growth of the community in this work. Avoid "gotcha" moments where people are punished for sharing their areas for growth.

There is no way around it: developing the level of trust needed for people to receive feedback on their growth around race and racism will take time. But prioritizing these elements consistently over time will help people feel supported while also understanding the expectations around assessment.

A Culture Based on Feedback

We have observed school cultures where sharing feedback with a supervisor or colleague opens the potential for a "gotcha" moment, and as a result, a number of educators choose not to share their feedback, particularly with their supervisors. Trust is essential to building a culture that collects and shares feedback. Even in school districts where collecting this data is required, trust is necessary. This is especially true when we are asking folks for feedback around race. In order to build trust with individuals, encourage them to focus on growing their practice with this information. When someone shares their thoughts with you, listen to them rather than voicing your own judgments. Additionally, you can collaboratively identify areas for growth.

As leaders, it is important that we encourage people not just to accept feedback but to apply it to their own work. As people become more comfortable sharing and receiving feedback, consider asking questions such as:

- How do you plan to apply this feedback in your practice?
- What is one piece of feedback that has helped you reflect on your own racial identity development?
- Is there feedback that helps you understand how your goals are impacting students of color in comparison to white students?

Group Feedback

As the school engages in dismantling race and racism, it is important that community members have the opportunity to provide feedback on the work of the school. As described above, this is a great opportunity to reaffirm your commitment to racial justice and equity and to help the community understand how your goals are connected to this commitment. Feedback should be tailored to help the school grow in this work. The questions must therefore go beyond the "Do you like this change or not" variety to delve more deeply into what is successful or not about the change. "Do you like this or not" questions can be very limiting, because racial bias can cloud individuals' responses. For example, consider the framing of the sample feedback questions below that address a goal of achieving more equitable homework.

Over the past year, our school has stopped giving students points for homework in their grades. This practice is in line with Joe Feldman's book *Grading for Equity* and in line with our core value of racial equity.

Sample Question 1: Do you like this change to the homework policy?

    a. Yes

    b. No

Sample Question 2: What is one way we can improve this policy?

    a. More opportunities for students to redo their homework.
    b. Clearer expectations that students should complete homework.
    c. More accountability for students who do not complete their homework.
    d. More valuable homework for students.
    e. Other: _____.

You'll note that for both sample questions, there is clarity about why the school is making this change and how it is tied to racial equity. However, sample question 2 is a more effective feedback tool than sample 1 because the answers provide more detailed information instead of a general opinion.

Because many families are used to the traditional structure of school that worked for some students, they are likely to respond that they do not like the policy change. This does not mean the school made the wrong decision in creating this change. Asking about the popularity of policy changes may simply reinforce the culture that already exists, rather than supporting efforts for effectual and meaningful change. If we want to empower the voices of historically marginalized people, we need to expand the school culture, not reaffirm the existing one. In schools trying to dismantle racism, resistance to change is inevitable, particularly from those with the most privileges. While it is important to get feedback, it is also important to get the feedback that's going to help you improve policy changes, not retreat to the inequitable system that already existed. Ultimately these changes are good for everyone.

Formal Evaluation

Formal evaluation is time-consuming and arduous. As practitioners, we have taken part in many formal evaluations when the results and recommendations were exactly what we thought they would be. ("We paid how much for them to tell us that?") However, formal evaluations address our biases; therefore, the result can instill confidence. This is critically important when there is a lack of trust from vulnerable populations. Imagine being a parent who feels silenced and listens to the school explain that "we took some feedback, and it sounds like we're doing a great job." Sometimes a formal process helps to build trust.

We experienced this sentiment when we decided to conduct an equity audit looking into our athletic program. Athletics is a very intense program where there are a lot of strong opinions when it comes to who makes a team or how players are treated. We had heard several concerns from BIPOC students, as well as from female and nonbinary students, about their experiences in the program and how they were treated by other teams, coaches, and officials. We believed a formal process such as an equity audit would help us conduct a thorough investigation, bring on advisors from the community, and report to many different groups. Through our equity audit, we were able to understand the experiences of students from traditionally marginalized groups and their families and work with our coaches and athletic department to become more culturally responsive.

While time-consuming, a formal evaluation process can be extremely helpful in assessing what work needs to be done and evaluating your work as an antiracist school. Here are some ideas to consider when conducting a formal evaluation.

- Create a transparent process. Communicate with your community the objectives and goals of the formal evaluation, as well as the conclusions. Consider sharing with key constituent groups, including those most impacted by the evaluation.
- Advisory group. We have found an advisory group to be helpful in giving us feedback as well as checking us on our progress. Consider including students, staff, and family members. Additionally, make sure you have diverse representation.
- Outside versus internal consultant. In our experience, schools may hire a consultant or use an external tool because it is easier. In equity work, easier does not mean better. Nevertheless, the benefit of a consultant doing this work is that they have experience and will most likely get the analysis completed sooner. The benefit to doing this process internally, though, is that you are building capacity so that you can continue to evaluate, and so you are able to develop questions that meet the needs of your individual culture. There are benefits to both, but make sure you are choosing the option that addresses your needs and does not impact your legitimacy.
- Thorough is better than fast. We all want answers immediately, but take your time. If you are doing this internally, it may take a lot longer than with an outside group. Be deliberate and thorough in your work.

Formal evaluation is an effective strategy in the same way that summative assessment helps us understand the entirety of our work. Consider using these processes as opportunities to track your progress in your racial equity work. This is the final part of the evaluation structure. Within these practices, you will need different tools to help you most effectively assess your work. The final section of this chapter discusses different assessment tools that you can use.

Differentiating the Assessment Tools

Here are some critical questions for helping you create the right tool for your community:

- What am I looking for?
- What is the most effective way to get the answers I need?
- What is the easiest and most efficient way to get these answers?
- What challenges exist?
- How do I ensure the voices of marginalized groups are equitably heard?

Individual Check-Ins

Meeting with individuals is perhaps the easiest way to assess the work that is being done. As school leaders, we need to move away from our offices and be present in the building to engage with students and staff. Furthermore, speaking with family members can be an important way to understand the context of their concern or support for a particular action.

As we find ourselves in more formal roles, such as principal, it can be difficult for people to speak their truth in conversation with us because of their fear of retribution or their focus on being respectful. But the more regularly you engage with your community, the more you can break down these barriers and build trust, allowing others to express their honest opinions.

In our work, there is nothing more valuable than one-on-one conversation. But these conversations can be overlooked in the fast-paced environment of our schools. Some ways to ensure you get this feedback include:

- Asking questions about actions, policies, or ideas during your informal conversations with people.
- Recognizing that people do not have a lot of time, so keep conversations short. Ask simple, general questions, such as, "Did

you see my newsletter message about incorporating restorative practices in our classrooms? What do you think about it?"

- Reinforcing your school's value of racial equity by being explicit about the racial equity work. "I think restorative practices could help our classrooms be more connected, especially if we focus on connecting with our students of color. How do you see us being able to do that?"

- Actively listening. These opportunities are less for you to speak and more for you to listen. Give your undivided attention.

It is important to have these one-on-one conversations with a variety of people. Sure, it feels good to meet with people who agree with your vision, but that will only create an echo chamber of validation for you. Check in with people who question this work or are unsure. What feedback do they have to help you think things through? Though they may be brief, if done regularly, these kinds of check-ins will help you assess the impact of the work.

Surveys

It is critical to develop surveys that get the information you are looking for. Who is your target audience? Are you looking for general feedback (good or bad) or specific feedback that will help guide you as you make changes? What are you going to do with the responses? These kinds of questions will help you think through how to formulate the right questions.

Here are a few resources we like to use to help develop survey questions:

- "Write Survey Questions" from the Pew Research Center: pewresearch.org/our-methods/u-s-surveys/writing-survey-questions

- *Using Equity Audits to Create Equitable and Excellent Schools* by Linda Skrla, Kathryn Bell McKenzie, and James Joseph Scheurich

- MAEC tools for equity audits: maec.org/res/tools/
- That qualitative research book you had to buy for grad school!

There have been times when we have used surveys to help us understand how the community is adapting to or using a change, instead of asking them whether they like the change or not. While we have received feedback from community members that they want to be able to tell us, "We don't like it," it's been more helpful to understand what is being done to incorporate or resist this action. For example, if you were incorporating more diverse texts into an English curriculum, it would be worth considering whether you are going to get more useful feedback if you ask "Do you like these books or not?" versus "What are some of the common themes you learned from these books?"

It is important to note that we are not against asking questions about whether people agree/disagree or like/dislike. It is important to hear a variety of opinions on a topic and to dipstick on public opinion. However, we find that too often, school leaders rely only on these questions and do not incorporate more substantive questions that will help them improve. In antiracist work, it is likely that people will push back against our changes, particularly those with the most privilege and power. Therefore, if we only rely on public opinion, we are going to make very little progress.

Focus Groups

Focus groups are a great formal strategy to understand the impact of this work and can be an excellent way to ascertain the students' viewpoints. We have set up meetings with students with a clear protocol and well-thought-out questions on the topic at hand. For example, when we were working to change our high school schedule, we met with several groups of students to walk them through different types of schedules and features we were considering. We made sure that our groups included a diverse range of students representing many facets of our school, based on such things as the kinds of courses they took, their family structure (paying attention to students who had additional responsibilities, worked after school, or took care of their siblings), their learning styles, and different types of disability. We also made sure we had racial diversity within these focus groups.

Quantitative Measures

When we use these tools to gather peoples' opinions, we can be inundated with data, which can be overwhelming for school leaders as well as other members of the school community. Identifying the quantitative data to focus on can be equally overwhelming. Ensuring that your goal is clear and focused will help you make sense of and use the data you have collected. For example, when we were assessing the racial disparity of our grading structure, we used our student information system to pull data from all grades based on racial groups. Additionally, when we wanted to understand the impact of increasing our mixed-level classes, we focused our data on the number of students who had access to honors classes. When we changed our grading system during the COVID-19 pandemic, concerned about the pandemic furthering existing disparity, we continued to track grades for these groups. This type of data collection was focused on a specific goal: narrowing the racial grade disparity in our school. We made sure to share the data with our staff and continue to monitor the data as we made the change. If you do not have a specific goal, you can become overwhelmed by the volume of data you have access to.

Equity Audits

An equity audit is a process that a school can follow to assess equity work being done within the community. Typically, equity audits are used as a more formal process to learn about our work. They can be large or small, can have a general focus or pinpoint a specific area of your school or work, and can incorporate many or only a few of the tools described. They can be done as the work begins and can be repeated as the work progresses. Equity audits should not be misconstrued as unruly behemoths that can overwhelm us and consume all of our time and energy, meaning they are therefore best avoided. Rather, we can make the process more manageable by scaling these audits to a size that is appropriate for the work we are doing. It is important that you use resources designed to help you with the specific issue you are evaluating. In some circumstances, we have used outside resources to guide us through the process. There are many free equity audit forms online. We recommend you search for resources created or recommended by reputable organizations, such as Learning for Justice. These resources can be helpful to use directly or as a reference to create your own. Generally, we have found these outside resources most helpful when doing a preliminary check on the equity in our schools.

Because equity audits are a more formal process than a one-off survey or informal conversation, they offer schools an opportunity to demonstrate how serious they are about addressing inequity. It is important to remember, however, that an equity audit alone is not a solution to addressing inequity; it is merely a way to gather more information and to assess your actions. Additionally, remember that these audits do not have to be so overwhelming that you avoid incorporating them into your assessment process. What matters is that you are mindful of the purpose of the equity audit and of what you are trying to learn from it, that the work is transparent, and that you develop a manageable process so that you can effectively find the answers you are looking for.

Conclusion

In the cycle of inquiry, assessment is a critical step to check the efficacy of our actions. Ultimately the question we should be asking during this process is: Are our actions working and for whom? When we look at this question through an antiracist lens, our goal is to build on the actions that are effectively dismantling racist structures and systems and revise or stop the actions that continue to uphold racist structures and systems. The more regularly we assess, the more we can learn. It is also important to remember that assessing is different from public-opinion polling. "Is this change working and for whom?" is a different question than "Do you like this change?" It is very plausible that some of our work is going to be effective in establishing equity but is also going to be very unpopular. This is why antiracist work is hard and messy. The remainder of this book will focus on how to build a culture that is willing to get into this work. In our experience, the better your school community understands that an antiracist school is good for all students, the more popular your actions will be.

KEY IDEAS

- Assessment is necessary for gauging progress, or lack thereof, and will help you cease actions that reinforce racial inequality and racism.
- Use informal and formal assessment strategies to regularly check your work and also conduct summative evaluations.
- Personal assessment strategies help you assess your own work and collaborate with trusted groups to provide you with feedback.
- Fostering an antiracist culture requires assessing others; consider both formal and informal strategies to assess how all members of the community are buying into this work.
- Consider using multiple tools for assessment to reduce the impact of bias.

CHANGE THE NARRATIVE

LEARN-Learn how to use different tools of assessment that can be used for different purposes to address antiracist practices, programs, and policies.

REFLECT-Conduct a self-assessment and identify areas of strength and areas for improvement. Think about what you will need to grow in these particular areas.

ACT-Work with your colleagues to implement an equity audit. Make sure you communicate the purpose of the audit and your plans to follow up.

ASSESS-Revisit progress on your intended goals frequently by speaking with multiple stakeholders, including supervisor, colleagues, students, and families.

PART II

LEADING AN
ANTIRACIST CULTURE

CHAPTER 6

LEADING TO DEFINE AN ANTIRACIST SCHOOL CULTURE

To be antiracist is to reject cultural standards and level cultural difference.

—IBRAM X. KENDI

The first half of this book focused on helping the school leader get acquainted with antiracist leadership and with utilizing the cycle of inquiry as a structure for their learning and development. Leaders serve as a model for others within the school community: in their commitment to learning about race and racism, their reflection on this learning and on their own participation within a racist system, their response to crises, and their strategic planning and assessment of their own work and the work within their school. Racism will never be dismantled with the work of just one person, however. Rather, it will require a fundamental shift to a culture that identifies the racist ideas and policies within the school and commits to changing them so that it can become a school that loves, supports, and fosters learning for ALL students. In the second part of this book, we turn to exploring how antiracist leaders can use these new-found skills to create an antiracist school culture.

"Where do we begin?" is a common question we are asked when we are invited to meet with school leaders who have come to a decision that it is time to do "something." That "something" usually follows an event: a racially charged school incident that has gone public (likely not for the first time), pressure from community advocacy groups to become an antiracist school, poor performance evaluations on school-wide goals for achieving equity and excellence for all students, or, what has become more common recently, a desire to join the national movement to address systemic racism after a litany of high-profile murders of unarmed Black individuals by police officers and vigilantes, as well as increasing hostility toward migrants, particularly those from Latin America, and rising anti-Asian racism in response to the COVID-19 pandemic.

Although it is the latter that has increased our invitations to work with school districts, it also reveals a performative desire to address an issue that deserves a bigger question than "Where do we begin?" In many ways, the question that is really being asked in these situations is "Where do we begin so that we can fix this problem immediately?" But dismantling racism is more complex and requires a more systemic cultural shift than other issues we might be used to addressing within our schools. The more productive question that everyone in the room should be asking is "Who do we want to become and what is getting in our way?"

When we think of culture, we automatically default to our experiences of our own cultural practices, whether it be how we celebrate, our beliefs about religion and spirituality, or our values about respect and work ethic. When a school community is dominated by members of one culture, particularly if the dominant group is white and homogeneous, that culture unconsciously becomes the standard and hierarchy for all to adapt to, leaving little room for the diverse values and beliefs that others may hold.

These cultural standards should be examined and revised to prioritize equity, inclusion, and representation for all students and the broader school community. The voice of leadership will be significant, as you will need to develop a platform that can project a vision for this work and reinforce both its necessity and your unrelenting commitment to it. It will require constant assessment of the current practices and structures that do not promote these ideals, and in most instances, a harsh criticism of them. To begin the antiracist journey, you must set the standard for this work as nonnegotiable and be prepared to identify other leaders to support this mission.

This chapter is intended to help you transition from developing your own skills as a school leader to encouraging the development of these skills in other members of the school community. It lays out the systems that are needed to begin to shift culture in your school so that you can become a school focused on antiracism.

Build a Leadership Team

One place to begin when creating an antiracist culture is to identify other school leaders on this quest and build a leadership team. Effective leaders recognize that they cannot do this work alone and that the power and influence in a school culture is distributed throughout the school. Therefore, a strategic leader will identify a leadership team that is committed to this work and is also influential with other people in the school. The role of your organization's leadership in this mission will be to serve as catalysts for positive change, and also to set the tone and hold the culture of antiracism as the standard, day in and day out. Leaders can be drawn from a number of individuals and groups in your school community. Often, we think of school administrators and principals as obvious choices, but you should also consider including those who are seen as cultural leaders in your school. It may be that you have to survey your community to discover who has taken an independent stance in this movement and subsequently established followers.

This inventory will lead you to educators who have shown a demonstrated commitment to social justice; student groups that have a pulse on the student experience and can speak on behalf of marginalized voices; parents who are active in your community and can mobilize other parents to participate. "Leaders participate equally as one of the many essential voices at the table. Given the opportunity to listen to and hear the creative ideas, hopes, and dreams of their colleagues and organization stakeholders, leaders recognize that their job is to plant the seed and nurture the best in others."[1] Leaders help to stimulate the change of your culture.

Once you have determined the leaders who will join you on this mission, find a set time for all to come together and develop a plan that considers staff development, student learning, and community outreach. This work is long-term but can be broken down into smaller goals and objectives (whether by week, month, or term) and should include a process to share frequent updates of your progress. Transparency with your staff around this plan and the intended goals is absolutely necessary, and your school leaders can help you establish the best methods of communication, whether emails, department meetings, school assemblies, newsletters, or all of the above, to make sure you are reaching the broadest audience.

It is most likely a mistake to view your leadership team as a fixed entity. In any given year, people leave positions or have personal crises, and new people become inspired. Make sure there are many off-ramps for people who need self-care and on-ramps for new people. We have found great allies and leaders in this work who just a year prior were skeptical or incurious about this work and then became more energized and engaged. These people can be extremely influential to others who also feel skeptical. As with any leadership challenge, when the same people lead this work every year, the team becomes disconnected and the work stagnates. Furthermore, expanding leadership opportunities helps to increase commitment to the work throughout your school.

Equally important is to build a team that is not homogeneous in race, gender, or roles, nor is solely made up of BIPOC staff. Too often, the responsibilities of this work fall to BIPOC staff members who may

---

1 David L. Cooperrider and Diana Whitney, *Appreciative Inquiry: A Positive Revolution in Change* (San Francisco: Berrett-Koehler, 2005).

already be burdened by the impact of continual microaggressions and isolation in your school community. The diversity of experiences and representation on your team will help you minimize unintentional missteps and avoid overlooking key standards and norms held by different groups.

Messaging

One of the key factors in moving this work forward is constant communication of your commitment to antiracism, your denouncement of racist acts, and updates on the work happening in your school community. As a school principal, the responsibility for communication and for providing guidance on when, how often, and in what format information should be delivered to reach multiple stakeholders falls heavily on you and your school leaders.

Whether it is sharing your entry plan, articulating your vision, addressing a crisis, or highlighting a success, communication is vital to help your school community understand why you are doing this work and what direction you are heading. As previously mentioned, many people see certain facets of racism as normal, or they never considered the inequity in certain areas. It is only when we have a clear communication strategy that you will be able to help the school community move forward with this work and to grow support for your actions.

Communication about race needs to be frequent. Many of us fall into the trap of only talking about race and racism during a crisis, when emotions run high, which does not lead to thoughtful and productive conversations. If you engage with the community about race and racism regularly, when intense moments do occur, you will be better prepared and will have developed some common language to talk about race.

Because regular communication helps to change the narrative, incorporate your antiracist leadership in all manner of formal communication with the community. Whether it is your opening-day message to staff, back to school night message to families, or newsletter or assembly with students, ensure you incorporate your message into all forms of formal communication. In crafting your opening-day messages, consider words to empower students to be active, demonstrate to families the goal of developing civically engaged students who stand up for others, and encourage educators in the critical need of personal reflection to help students. Some leaders may argue that this communication is performative and superficial, but every time you formally reach out to the community, you are sharing your vision and its purpose in hope of conveying the importance of this work to the community.

Your formal communications can incorporate videos, articles, and other resources to help support your narrative. School leaders can deliver live or prerecorded video messages, include links to articles from credible local and national news media, and create a resources page on your school's website to provide easy access to resources, books, and training to support educators and parents in having further conversations about race. We recommend the articles "Teaching Young Children about Race" and "Raising Race-Conscious Children: How to Talk to Kids About Race and Racism" and the websites EmbraceRace and Learning for Justice.[2] There are many additional resources to consider that can best align with your community makeup and needs.

Most importantly, different groups of people will receive communication differently. Make sure you are tailoring communication directly for your traditionally marginalized groups. Don't wait, expecting them to come to you; you need to seek them out. This is equity work. We'll spend more time talking about different strategies to engage with communities of color in the later chapters.

---

2 Louise Derman-Sparks and Julie Olsen Edwards, "Teaching Young Children about Race: A Guide for Parents and Teachers," Teaching for Change, October 21, 2021, teachingforchange. org/teaching-about-race; Beata Mostafavi, "Raising Race-Conscious Children: How to Talk to Kids about Race and Racism," *Children's Health*, Michigan Medicine, July 22, 2020, healthblog.uofmhealth.org/childrens-health/raising-race-conscious-children-how-to-talk -to-kids-about-race-and-racism; EmbraceRace, embracerace.org/; Learning for Justice, learningforjustice.org.

Informal Communication

While our formal communication is important, we can also make significant strides in changing the narrative through our day-to-day interactions. The more often we can have authentic conversations about this work, the more we can move people. Typically, these informal communications occur with individuals or small groups. Each of these small conversations gives you the opportunity to build upon your larger narrative, and they can also empower others to act. There is no replacing the success we get from one-on-one conversations. These conversations take a lot of time, but they are the most effective way to move the larger conversation. And always remember to listen.

Make a Statement

Many schools and institutions across the country have released statements to demonstrate support for equality and denounce racism. However, these statements miss condemning the specific acts and structures of racism that impede progress. They also lack an actual plan to dismantle these same acts and structures within their own organizations.

As a school leader, you want your strong statement to include 1) a clear denouncement of racism and acknowledgment of its prevalence and harm, 2) a long-term commitment to working toward being an antiracist school, and 3) steps you will take to begin addressing the issue(s).

Overall, your comfort and clarity in communication is critical to the impact of this work. Developing a common language that your community can adopt and fall back on when questions arise may be helpful. This can also provide support for staff when they want to better understand how to frame their conversations and develop more comfort in their own communication.

Manage Resistance

It is equally important to identify where you have experienced or anticipate dissent. Understanding your school culture also means that you recognize those who are opposed to change—who are comfortable with the status quo. This is not to amplify their voices, but to understand the root of their resistance. This is where surveys or focus groups can help solicit feedback from your school community about concerns, fears, and barriers. Oftentimes, resistance stems from lack of information, miscommunication, or fear of the unknown.

You and your team can share the responsibility for engaging staff and community in reiterating your school's mission and values of antiracism and providing accurate and consistent information about the intended goals of your decisions. Regardless of pushback and resistance, leadership must consistently reinforce that this work is nonnegotiable and that there is no room for tolerance of hate and harm in the school community. Be prepared to stand firm when resistance presents itself from disgruntled staff and griping parents.

Inclusion

Diversity is often centered in conversations about antiracism and prioritized as a goal in the work, as it should be. But it is also important to move beyond *diversity*—the "presence of difference"—and embrace *inclusion*—"the practice of providing everyone with equal access to opportunities" and a sense of belonging.[3] Inclusion honors the diversity in your school community by offering voice, space, and command to historically marginalized members. It is not enough to invite difference into the room if the voices of difference do not feel heard or valued as leaders and authorities in the desired culture shift.

To be inclusive, you must always question who is being centered in your decision-making. Our cultural standards have made it easy for

---

3 "Diversity + Inclusion," Built In, accessed February 5, 2022, builtin.com/diversity-inclusion.

us to believe that our own educational experiences—the status quo in education—reflect the only way to determine and assess learning objectives and progress. Most of these assessments have been centered in the whiteness of our instruments, tools, materials, and norms. By bringing a diversity of voices into the room and centering their experiences, you will hear that many of these instruments and norms had adverse effects, causing people to feel excluded from their own learning.

Reflecting on her experience as a young Black student in a predominantly white school, Kathy recalls that her culture and norms were never a part of the conversation, never mind that teachers never centered her in the classroom. This forced her to assimilate to a learning style and environment that never included teachers that looked like her, and did not have the language or curriculum to address her own cultural norms and historical references outside of the school system. The message she internalized was that her way was wrong, and that success was achieved through assimilation to white standards.

This is the message carried by students of color who are implicitly told they don't matter because their voices are not invited or respected. Inclusion must take into consideration *all* differences, even if that difference makes up only a small percentage of your school community. It requires that you seek out opportunities to center diverse voices, regardless of the discomfort this gives to those who see this work as unnecessary or lacking value because they are accustomed to *their* voices being centered. The work of antiracism is to dismantle exclusion as a cultural standard and embrace the commitment to inclusion as an ultimate goal.

Conclusion

This work of creating an antiracist school culture will be challenging, but your first step is to ask yourself in reference to your school community, "Who do we want to become?" Identify where value is placed and consider who benefits from those values and who is often left behind. Once you are firm in your purpose, set your focus on creating a culture that seeks out leaders and partners, reiterates unwavering commitment, amplifies marginalized voices as experts, communicates your mission continually, and holds your community members accountable. Through these actions, you will build a strong foundation for transformational change, allowing you to begin transitioning from considering your own growth as an antiracist leader to building an antiracist school community. One of the critical first steps of a strong antiracist culture is a strong culture of adults committed to this work.

KEY IDEAS

- Cultural standards need to be examined and revised to prioritize equity, inclusion, and representation for all students and the broader school community.
- Your school's leadership team can support you in your communication and realizing your vision.
- A sense of urgency rarely produces sustainable change—transformational change requires a commitment of ongoing learning and discomfort in conversations and in practice.
- Ongoing communication about your vision and plan to all community stakeholders is essential.

CHANGE THE NARRATIVE

LEARN–Prioritize inclusion by seeking out voices of students and staff of color to identify needs and prioritize planning.

REFLECT–Think about other school staff who serve as positive-change catalysts to support the idea that this work is necessary and nonnegotiable. What leadership role could they play to support this work?

ACT–Demonstrate unwavering commitment through consistency and using multiple communication modes.

ASSESS–Use existing quantitative and qualitative data to assess the negative impact of current practices and structures.

CHAPTER 7

ANTIRACIST COLLEGIALITY

The level of collective courage in an organization is the absolute best predictor of that organization's ability to be successful.

—BRENÉ BROWN

Throughout this book, we cover many topics about fostering an antiracist culture. While our focus is always on how to create a culture where students feel loved so that they can learn, this kind of school can only exist if the adults also feel loved, so they can learn from and support one another. Without a doubt, the way the leader interacts with other adults is critical in setting the tone, and the importance of fostering antiracist adult interactions should not be underestimated. Regardless of how visible leaders appear within the building, most staff interactions will occur without school leaders' presence. Dynamic leaders need to consider how to support an antiracist staff culture that will continue even when they are not present.

The hardest work we have to do to move a culture is change behaviors and practices. Colleagues are extremely influential in shaping an educator's opinions and feelings. Additionally, unless teachers are regularly observing each other, most educators develop their opinions about each other through their social interactions and what they hear from students. The greatest source of learning for educators is what they learn from each other, especially from the teachers they trust the most.[1] Many times we have heard a teacher describe a colleague as one of the most influential teachers in the school, only to discover they have formed this opinion based on limited information overheard from students and other colleagues. This is not meant to discredit those perceptions, but rather to emphasize how influential collegiality is in a school.

This function of teacher collegiality can be challenging because ideas are formulated based on perception rather than information or research. This is particularly problematic when we think about race and racism, where a teacher's racial biases can influence others. As a result, if we are to effectively change the narrative, then a tremendous focus on how educators interact and support each other is critical work for a leader.

This chapter will focus on how to foster strong antiracist collegiality. There are crucial areas to pay attention to, especially with majority white faculties, which encompasses the vast majority of schools. We should also be prepared for strong opinions about holding on to the school's existing traditions and culture, which can be exacerbated by suspicion toward administrators. While most educators are concerned about inequities in their school, some may freeze and resist when asked to make a change. Remember, teaching is always personal; it is never business. Therefore, helping educators see their own bias and contributions to racism can be extremely challenging, let alone asking them to change their practice to address these biases.

Furthermore, the more we are successful in diversifying our faculty, the more tradition and faculty culture shifts. This places pressure on what veteran educators traditionally found safe or reliable. Be prepared for comments such as "this place isn't like it used to be" and understand the layers that exist in these comments, particularly as the faculty changes. Shifts away from traditional teaching will most likely

---

1 Kenneth A. Frank et al., "Social Capital and the Diffusion of Innovations within Organizations: The Case of Computer Technology in Schools," *Sociology of Education* 77, no. 2 (2004): 148–71, doi.org/10.1177/003804070407700203.

upset and even anger staff members, which can affect other staff members depending on their social capital throughout the faculty.

At the same time, there will be colleagues who jump on board with this work quickly or who are already leading the way. These colleagues can be the most influential people to help push against negative feelings surrounding change. It is through these people that we can find opportunities to expand into antiracist work.

Students remain in school for only a few years. Some families may have multiple children and be a part of the school community for longer. But educators stay within a school community for ten, twenty, sometimes forty years. As educators, we are the heart and soul of the school culture. If we are to foster an antiracist culture, we need to invest in antiracist collegiality and help educators understand that racism exists even among their networks and systems of work. With this understanding, educators can commit to learning from each other, supporting their colleagues, and amplifying the voices of their colleagues of color.

Questions educators can ask themselves to understand their role in becoming a more antiracist colleague:

1. How often do I try to answer questions about race on my own before I reach out to a colleague of color?
2. How often do I check in with and listen to colleagues of color during emotionally hard times?
3. How often do I listen to colleagues of color about their opinion without responding or speaking over them?
4. How often do I advocate for or amplify the voice of a colleague of color and make sure they get the credit they deserve?
5. What kinds of compliments do I provide colleagues of color? Are they consistent with the compliments I provide white colleagues? Is my tone consistent?

The work of creating an antiracist staff culture includes fostering a collaborative culture focused on dismantling racism, leveraging preexisting structures such as professional learning communities and unconferences so that they center race and racism, and ensuring that staff of color is not only supported but set up to thrive in our schools. Fostering antiracist collegiality requires a staff-focused strategy that encourages every educator to be engaged in strengthening the adult culture.

Collaboration

Fostering a collaborative culture is a crucial step to moving a school forward. At the same time, antiracist leaders must be aware of the racial dynamics and power structures within staff collaboration so that both staff of color and antiracist perspectives are heard and have influence. With that, leaders need to separate collaboration from autonomous work. While offering autonomy is critical to allowing educators to innovate, structured collaboration is essential to ensuring a consistent focus on antiracist work, where we hold each other accountable and learn with each other, and where power structures can be addressed. Therefore, antiracist collaboration needs to address racial power dynamics among colleagues and focus on dismantling racism in the classroom.

Random versus Intentional Grouping

As we see with students, staff prefer to choose their own groups during meetings. But when we support this option, they are prone to work with those like them—whether it is their friends, fellow grade/subject matter teachers, office mates, and so on. Unsurprisingly, this tends to lead to less diverse groupings and more groupthink.

Diverse teams are smarter and better able to prevent groupthink. They also push against the power dynamic that can exist when too many people with the same perspective and same experience dominate the conversation. We've all had colleagues who dominate the conversation in a group while others remain silent. Being mindful of the group structure will help address these issues.

Instead of allowing staff to choose their own groups during faculty meetings and professional development, consider being intentional about diversifying groups. Two options to do this are to create your own grouping or to randomize groups. There are advantages to each of these strategies. If you create your own groupings, you can separate groups based on levels of experience, bring together proponents and detractors, or diversify the vocal and the quiet, for example. However, be aware that staff will pick up on this strategy quickly, and relying only on this method can create challenges around trust.

You certainly have less choice when you randomize groups; however, it creates more heterogeneity than allowing staff to choose their own groups. In our experience, people tend to prefer this strategy over administrator-chosen groupings.

Ultimately, we would suggest that you regularly change up the grouping strategy. Over time you will know the right structure for the needs of the work. What is important is that you are mindful of educators forming their own groups. While we all prefer to be with our friends when we are asked to form a group, this is precisely the problem when we get involved with work around race. It is always our hope that when we do allow groups to form on their own, over time we will see staff looking to work with people they don't know or who think or look different than they do. This is a sign of collaborative progress. Once the groups have been formed, consider the importance of common norms and agreements for all groups.

Racial Affinity Groups

Affinity groups are a great place to support the voices of people of color in your school. As with student affinity groups, faculty benefit from safe spaces with people who look like them in order to support each other and feel validated in their experiences. It can be exhausting for traditionally marginalized groups to work in a setting in which they experience daily microaggressions and, at times, overt racism, which can ultimately lead to isolation, exclusion, and a lack of community. Providing affinity spaces for support and safety will allow them to recharge, connect with people who share the same experiences, and find a sense of security in their group. This section describes how to develop affinity groups for people of color and our experiences with white-only affinity spaces.

Affinity Groups for People of Color

A few years back a teacher of color hosted an affinity group for educators of color. The intent of the group was to reflect on the year, eat and relax together, and discuss some of their common experiences being a person of color at the high school. When discussing the outcomes of the meeting, the facilitator shared some of the common themes that emerged from the retreat. Overall, the group felt it was beneficial just to be together outside of school to recharge. We have continued to support these meetings and expanded them throughout our school district. What has ensued is a supportive collaboration among staff members who share a common experience—being a person of color in a majority white faculty.

Over time and as the diversity of the faculty has expanded, this group has expanded, too. We now have multiple affinity groups throughout the school district for different groups of educators—for example, an administrator affinity group and an elementary educator affinity group and a secondary educator affinity group. What we have learned is that, above all, these groups have given staff a chance to refresh, but we have also found that staff of color have started to feel more comfortable speaking up at faculty meetings and taking on leadership and other exciting work. While we believe that some of these outcomes are connected to forming this affinity space and the other work we are doing around racism, ultimately this group remains focused on being a safe space for educators to connect.

As director of diversity, equity, and inclusion in a large school district, Kathy recognized there are limited opportunities to engage with staff in other buildings and took the opportunity to create the district-wide affinity space for all staff of color. Bringing these colleagues together several times a year allows them not only to connect and share their experiences and support one another, but also gives them networking and mentorship opportunities to support career advancement and to share strategies in support of inclusion, diverse curriculum, and school-based activities. The hope of these spaces is that the organic connections staff of color make will help them feel less isolated and more efficacious in their work, and that this will support efforts to retain staff and faculty of color.

To legitimize this plan and ensure consistency, we requested and received funding to compensate identified facilitators who would carry the work of planning and organizing events. This funding speaks to a crucial issue as schools and districts take on antiracist work—valuing people of color.

The Value of People of Color Leading Equity Work

As schools and organizations take on antiracist work, it becomes increasingly clear that there is a reliance on the people of color in the district to lead this work. People of color are the obvious choice because, as we have stated before, their racial identity development tends to be more advanced than their white colleagues. However, many districts consider leading this work to be an honor—a leadership and learning opportunity for the individual. As a result, many people of color are asked to take on this work for free. It has been our experience that many do end up doing this work for free because they are thrilled the district is finally interested in racial equity and because they are passionate about it. Don't fall into this trap. Schools and districts that believe in this work need to put money into it.

By expanding these affinity groups, we have been able to systematize a level of support for people of color in the district. The benefits to this work are retention, recruitment, and overall job satisfaction for people of color.

Learning Spaces for White Educators

As we have supported affinity spaces for different groups, we have also seen attempts by white educators to create white-only affinity spaces. Oftentimes, this request has come across our desk with good intentions—to give white educators a safe space to grow in their own racial identity, to talk about how to support students and colleagues of color, and to make mistakes without the guilt or embarrassment they would feel in front of their colleagues of color.

We have gone back and forth on this topic, as it is important for white educators who are entering this work to have spaces to learn and process without creating harm toward colleagues of color. Sometimes, the revelation of the existence and impact of racism by white people can be triggering to people of color who have experienced it their whole lives. Imagine being a person of color who has been reminded of their race daily and to be in a room full of white colleagues who, for the first time, are realizing their impact when they ignore race.

Still, while there are many people who do antiracist work who do value white-only affinity groups, in our experience, affinity spaces are for those who experience marginalization due to their identities representing a minority group within the community. A white-only space runs counter to the intention of creating an antiracist culture because it reinforces an exclusive group for the dominant culture. In many schools where the faculty are majority white, a faculty meeting is commonly experienced as an affinity space, as are most other spaces in the building. Therefore, creating additional spaces for white educators that exclude others feels counterintuitive.

We have also observed too many white-only affinity spaces that reinforce the dominant white culture, either through racist comments or the creation of inequitable structures due to lack of representation of ideas from those with lived experiences of exclusion. During training and workshops, it could make sense to create opportunities for white educators to have space to process with a skilled facilitator, while educators of color are offered the same opportunity, yet each group with different goals. Affinity spaces for people of color can provide moments of validation, reassurance, mentorship, and more.

For white educators, facilitated learning spaces (preferably not called affinity spaces) should be designed to go deeper into a new idea or concept, with full intention of self-reflection and commitment toward an antiracist culture. It must also be said that these groups should always return to the broader group and continue to listen to others and not rush to make decisions without the input and collaboration of those they intend to support. Ally or co-conspirator groups are an alternative that invites people of color but is geared toward educators who are newer to this work, most of whom will be white.

These groupscan be set up with the specific purpose of dismantling racism and empowering people of color in the school. Even still, these groups need to be designed in a way that encourages individuals to keep their privilege in check. It has been our experience that these groups organize with a lack of awareness of the privilege and power they possess, which can lead them to stomping on the voices and ideas of people of color because they are unaware. Additionally, they can fall into the trap of thinking they need to "win the antiracist Olympics" by casting judgment on other colleagues for not being as antiracist as they are.

Helping white educators in learning spaces remain focused on their goals is key to minimizing the potential to drift off into other projects and priorities. It is helpful to hold regular meetings and to develop specific plans to engage with students, families, and faculty of color and to consider how to amplify those voices, rather than amplify their own. As leaders, it is also healthy to reflect on power dynamics and set a cultural standard that discomfort can be a valuable characteristic of growth and reflection toward strengthening the community.

Antiracist white educators are essential to making this work successful. They are critical models for white colleagues who are just entering this work, and provide spaces for others to be challenged based on their level of racial identity development. It is important to remember that racial identity development should always be challenging and uncomfortable, but the challenge should align with the development level of each individual educator.

Supporting collaborative groups based on one's racial identity development, rather than a white-only affinity group, is a more effective strategy to support those just beginning this work. While these groups may tend to be majority white, they prevent the framing of a "white affinity group," which is high risk, low reward. This strategy also supports the development of people of color who are just entering this work.

Note on Staff of Color Just Beginning This Work

It is important to note that it is a false assumption that all people of color have a high level of racial identity development, as well as the skillset of an antiracist educator. Too often, faculty of color who are just beginning antiracism work are overly criticized because they do not yet have these skills. This in itself is racist thinking. Therefore, we want to be cautious with this note, because we have too often seen others overemphasize the challenges of staff of color who are developing their racial identity.

Some staff with limited racial identity development may be resistant to antiracist changes because they are among the few who have succeeded in the white dominant culture. Instead, they support the bootstrap concept—"I worked hard, therefore other people of color should work hard, as well." This is simply racist thinking.

Conclusion

Author Robin DiAngelo created a video in which she shared that "kindness alone will not end racism."[2] She was pushing back on the notion many of us learn as children—and may still believe—which suggests it is enough just to be kind to other people. Antiracist work is hard, it is emotional, and it is going to anger some people. To succeed requires a commitment from all educators to take the risk of taking on this work. It is critical that our colleagues interact with each other if we are to survive. It cannot be done by a savior, but rather by the collaboration of every adult who is committed to this work and to structures for collaboration, a balance of autonomy, and a shared vision. Staff of color should be provided affinity spaces, and white colleagues opportunities for learning about what it means to stand up for antiracism. School leaders are responsible for creating and sustaining a culture that continues to grow and improve. Kindness alone will not end racism. A fractured culture won't solve it either. In the next chapter, we look at how we can use evaluation and professional development to support teachers as they continue their individual journeys toward creating antiracist classrooms.

KEY IDEAS

- Fostering antiracist collegiality requires a staff-focused strategy that encourages every educator to be engaged to strengthen the adult culture.
- Racial affinity groups allow for staff of color to recharge, connect with people who share the same experiences, and find safety in their group.

---

2 Robin DiAngelo, interview by Michel Martin, *Amanpour & Co.*, PBS, August 3, 2021, pbs.org/wnet/amanpour-and-company/video/robin-diangelo-on-nice-racism/.

- Rather than white-only affinity groups, consider supporting co-conspirator groups that will be majority white but open to all and will focus on dismantling racism.

CHANGE THE NARRATIVE

LEARN–Discover the importance of bringing your staff and educators together to learn, process, and support each other.

REFLECT–How do preexisting collaboration structures work in your school? What inequities exist?

ACT–Host an "unconference" on race and racism. Empower those who are most passionate in your school to facilitate.

ASSESS–Survey staff about race relations among colleagues. Consider inviting the teachers' union and/or human resources to work with you.

CHAPTER 8

THE ANTIRACIST INSTRUCTIONAL LEADER

Education must begin with the solution of the teacher-student contradiction, by reconciling the poles of contradiction so that both are simultaneously teachers and students.

—PAULO FREIRE

As supervisors, we are always finding the appropriate tension: the more we seek to standardize, the more teachers resist, but the less we supervise, the more issues go unaddressed. Teachers have a lot of autonomy in their classrooms; therefore, the most effective instructional leadership environments are when teachers are eager to learn, willing to take risks, and committed to collaborating with others. When we are effective, supervision is focused on growth and usable feedback. In the same way we want teachers to use assessments as opportunities for students to learn, supervision should be viewed as an opportunity for professional learning and growth. The more we can coach and focus on educator growth, the more we can energize our staff. At the same time, antiracist leadership is also about addressing culturally insensitive practices that create inequitable experiences for students, detrimental classroom structures, and other forms of systemic racism in the classroom. Therefore, antiracist leadership and antiracist classroom practices are inextricably linked. Effective instructional leadership occurs when there is a coherence between the schoolwide vision and educator goals. As antiracist educators, race should be a driving part of this work.

The influence of the supervisor to shift teaching and learning should not be overlooked. Through observations and regular conversations, we are able to help educators think through their goals. As we make antiracist practices a part of our conversations, we then help embed them into the culture. Then, through collaboration, educator discussion helps to shift the culture. Like the Systems Thinking, Systems Changing game described in chapter 4, instruction shifts occur through systematic planning and action.

While supervision can help change the narrative, the absence of instructional supervision can allow a culture to develop on its own— one with inequitable structures and inconsistent experiences for students. Some educators rely on their preconceived notions of effective teaching and learning, while others buy into the notion that they can shut the door and do what they want. As we explained previously, when 80 percent of teachers are white, the culture created is likely one driven by the norms of white dominant culture. When we do not focus on instruction, students of color experience a classroom that was not set up for them. As a result, we can sometimes observe practice in majority BIPOC classrooms where the instruction is more authoritarian, more disciplinarian, and more focused on rule following than learning. Therefore, as supervisors with an antiracist mindset, we need to become more cognizant of how to help educators become antiracist teachers focused on building antiracist skills so that students feel seen and loved and expectations are high.

This work begins with creating an environment that encourages self-reflection about race and racism, provides effective professional learning opportunities around culturally responsive instruction, is open and honest about effective practices to engage a diverse range of students, and is driven toward improvement. This chapter will discuss how our supervisory role can institute antiracist practices to ensure teachers are growing in their practice as antiracist educators and how professional learning cycles can move educator practice forward.

We Gotta Talk about Race

It may come as no surprise to school leaders that educators, in large part, care about racial justice. In one study, 84 percent of educators indicated an interest in teaching an antiracist curriculum. But that same study found that only 14 percent of educators felt they had the resources or professional development to do so.[1] Considering educators grew up in the same educational system as our students, it is understandable that such a low percentage feel prepared. With so many educators interested in learning about antiracist teaching, we should help them understand that the work requires substantial self-work as described in the first part of the book, but we should also create the professional learning structure for this work to happen. Progress will not happen if we expect educators to work on their racial identity on their own.

As discussed in chapter 2, racial identity development is a critical part of your journey as an antiracist leader, and it is equally important to your educators' journeys, as well. One of the first steps we took to engage with our faculty was to have them learn about their own racial identity development. We wanted a baseline to make sure that all educators were able to identify where they were with their racial identity. With the district's support, we pulled twenty-five teachers and counselors out of the classroom for a one-day training on racial identity led by two teachers with experience in this work. The goal was to provide this training regularly once or twice over the school year. The project moved slowly at first, as there was trepidation around the topic. Additionally, for many people, looking inward was very difficult; they had a much easier time looking at systemic racism externally than

---

1 EdWeek Research Center, "Anti-Racist Teaching: What Educators Really Think," *Education Week*, September 25, 2020, edweek.org/leadership/anti-racist-teaching-what-educators-really-think/2020/09.

at their own contributions to creating a racist school culture. But it is only when individuals begin to reflect on their own practice that we are able to make strides.

Although this training moved slowly, it ran parallel to the other work we were doing as a faculty—including developing culturally responsive instruction and addressing racist incidents. Therefore, the constant conversation on race—as well as the events happening nationally—began to increase peoples' desire and willingness to engage in this work. We also added summer workshops, where the district provided principals money to pay educators to attend. Slowly the participation rate began to pick up.

Our school district also offered a yearly conference on race and achievement that allowed educators to provide and attend workshops on topics ranging from building representation in the curriculum, supporting multiracial students, and learning techniques for understanding disparities in the classroom. Over time, the topic of race became more commonly addressed in our professional work.

It was this continual work that allowed individuals to begin the cycle of inquiry that enabled them to reflect on their own role in the racist system. Sometimes they reflected on challenging interactions they had had with a student of color, sometimes they would comment on a teaching practice they picked up from a book that we purchased for the staff, or would ask for a recommendation for a book on race. At other times, they would seek us out to have a conversation about some aspect of race they were thinking about.

Over a few years of building a culture focused on racial identity awareness, in which people moved at their own pace, some taking longer than others, ultimately, a culture began to emerge that held antiracism at its core. It was very exciting to see this awareness develop among the teaching staff. However, supervising and evaluating educators at so many different levels of racial identity development, who often feel extremely vulnerable when speaking on this topic, continues to be challenging. Here again, we see the need for balance. Coming down too hard on the educators who need more time would shut them down, and offering them the continual encouragement they need to get comfortable with being uncomfortable and continue to grow is essential.

As the educators in our school began to reflect on their racial identity, they also began to feel more comfortable being vulnerable about which of their techniques are effective and which are not. This allowed us to engage more about positive and negative impacts on our students of color. With this vulnerability, evaluation became more collaborative and goal setting more authentic.

Curricular and Instructional Leadership

When it comes to leadership around racial justice, it is important to remind the community of the vision to maintain a focus on the importance of this work. A tension in this work is that we want to engage in it every moment of every day, but at the same time, we have to understand that it is long-term work and we do not want educators burning out. So, while educators need vision, support, and resources from an instructional leader, they also need time to improve, make mistakes, and identify what works. We have found that a clear message, consistent focus on antiracism, and time to innovate is the secret sauce to help educators evolve their practice. We have been asked by other schools how we have been able to make such progress in this work as a school. It is a challenging question because the solution lies in all the small conversations, collaborations, innovative ideas, and sharing of practices over the course of many years. It is easy to look back and see progress but, at the same time, still feel like there is so much work to do. But in looking back, we can see that there is one concept that has helped us continue to grow: a consistent focus on dismantling racism in and out of the classroom.

Culturally Responsive Instruction

Culturally responsive instruction is founded on the idea that the educator is committed to learning about the culture of every student and adapting their instructional practices to allow students' cultural strengths to shine. This lens of instruction is student-centered and antiracist. Though we cannot offer a full review of culturally responsive instruction in the context of this book, we highlight a few points for antiracist leaders to consider in this area.

One of the easiest mistakes we can make when trying to incorporate culturally responsive instruction is to confuse it for simply incorporating more diversity into our content. Culturally responsive instruction does not necessarily mean more diversity. We have come across educators who quickly jump to thinking they will support their students of color better if they include content about people of color. While it is important for students to see themselves in the curriculum, when this is the only change made, it can come off as hollow. Students need to know that we understand who they are as individuals, that we are curious about their cultures, and that we are willing to adjust our instruction based on their needs.

Culturally responsive instruction helps educators to understand their students so that students can engage and learn the curriculum. Culturally responsive instruction is a student-centered approach that supports choice as a way to engage students in the material. Approaches such as project-based learning and universal design for learning can support a culturally responsive lens, because we are responding to our students' diverse needs. However, they are not inherently culturally responsive. We need to understand the cultural needs of our students before we incorporate a response. Additionally, leaders can help educators incorporate culturally responsive instruction and move away from teaching strategies they use simply because they like them. The purpose of instruction is to help students to learn. Therefore, the instructional strategies we incorporate need to respond to the needs of students rather than be enjoyable to the educator.

Culturally Responsive Instruction

One study on culturally responsive instruction identified the following factors as having a positive impact on student learning:

- Respect for the legitimacy of different cultures;
- Empowering students to value all cultures, not just their own;
- Incorporating cultural information *into* the curriculum, instead of simply adding it on;
- Relating new information to students' life experiences;
- Teaching to the "whole child" and treating the classroom like a community;
- Addressing a spectrum of learning styles;
- Maintaining high expectations for student success.[2]

Social Justice Skills

Helping all educators find value in culturally responsive instruction is possible, but getting all educators to consider how their curriculum is connected to race and racism can be more challenging. In our experience there can be push back from teachers who think their curricular area does not lend itself to talking about racism. Interestingly, we have observed different subject departments in different schools with different perspectives about whether their curriculum is relevant to race and racism. We have observed math departments and history departments leading this work in some schools, and those same departments in others insisting their course or curriculum is not relevant. We have also heard from across the curricular spectrum: "I would love to teach more about race, but I don't have time in my curriculum." All of this pushback speaks more to fear than anything else. No matter what the curriculum is, every teacher has the potential to engage with culturally

---

2 Adapted from "Culturally Responsive Curriculum at a Glance," Learning for Justice, July 7, 2009, learningforjustice.org/magazine/culturally-responsive-curriculum-at-a-glance.

responsive instruction once they are committed to understanding the overlap in the work.

When we observe curricular departments leading in this work, they have typically moved their focus onto learning outcomes and skill development, rather than racing through content. By focusing on skill development, such as critical thinking, problem-solving, and research skills, our content opens up our curriculum to incorporate race as well as other social issues. Newton North World Language Department Chair Nancy Marrinucci regularly says, "In World Language, we can teach any topic, so long as it is in the target language."

One way to help educators see the overlap is to focus on social justice skills. Learning for Justice identified a list of social justice skills and created a scaffolded vertical alignment for each skill outcome.[3] In our district Antiracist Curriculum and Instruction Committee, we are prioritizing the following social justice skills from the Learning for Justice standards to align our learning outcomes for grades pre-K through 12, just as we would math or social studies standards:

- Students will recognize that people's multiple identities interact and create unique and complex individuals.
- Students will respectfully express curiosity about the history and lived experiences of others and will exchange ideas and beliefs in an open-minded way.
- Students will analyze the harmful impact of bias and injustice on the world, historically and today.
- Students will speak up with courage and respect when they or someone else has been hurt or wronged by bias.

We have found success having teachers identify how their curriculum area is connected to these skills. This then enables teachers to help their students develop or reinforce these skills. This can also be applied to entire school districts to develop this kind of vertical alignment

---

3 "Social Justice Standards," Learning for Justice, learningforjustice.org/frameworks/social
-justice-standards.

across schools, as well. Through this work we can ensure that all students in every classroom are focusing on antiracist work.

Supervision and Evaluation

As supervisors, we can stifle teacher growth when we focus on speed rather than effectiveness. It is true that we need to make decisions about a new teacher's potential in a short period of time, but if we are unclear on how an educator should improve, we can slow down their progress.[4] In the same way that a teacher can overwhelm a student by filling the margins of a student's essay with comments, so too can we overwhelm educators when our feedback is scattered all over the place. Therefore, our message for educators should be straightforward, consistent, and focused on growth.

As supervisors, we need to find the right balance between coaching and patience. Educators need to know that taking on antiracist and culturally responsive practices is critical to our work as a school, but they also need the space to innovate, try new practices, reflect, and grow.

We also want them to have the space to collaborate and share ideas. Critical friends groups and professional learning communities focused on this work provide educators with safe spaces to share ideas and receive feedback from colleagues. This type of collaboration can help educators feel supported and know they are not alone.

At the same time, when it comes to focusing on race, supervisors need to check educators' work to make sure good intentions are not having negative impacts on students. Imagine you walk into a classroom and you observe:

- A simulation of plantation life where students are playing roles of slave and master.

---

4 In Massachusetts, it is three years before teachers receive additional job protection called "professional teacher status."

- A teacher who offers up a debate among students about whether the N-word should be read aloud as they read *Huckleberry Finn* as a class.
- An environmental science book that praises the work of the early conservationists and downplays that of Indigenous people.
- A student presentation on immigration and housing that calls for "building more ghettos."

Situations like these are all too common, and they can go unnoticed or ignored. That is why it is critical we are proactive with professional development, to reduce the possibility these situations will arise, and we can help address them, as well. Situations like these are harmful to students in their understanding of race and particularly harmful for students of color and their sense of safety in the classroom.

It is quite possible that the educator's intention in all these situations was to help address racism, and that they felt unprepared and were unaware of the impact on students of color. While it may be common for these situations to be ignored or missed by administrators, we also can react in unconstructive ways when we are quick to punish or lose our temper with the educator. As leaders of color, we could see ourselves being easily triggered in one of these situations, which would impact our initial reactions if we came across them. When we are most effective as leaders, however, we acknowledge the harm, we are curious about the intention, and we help the educator grow so that they improve in this work.

Focusing on educator growth is a multistep and long-term project. Proactive professional learning helps to name the priority and pushes educators to reflect on their practice, lesson design, and cultural proficiency. We have read books—for example, *Culturally Responsive Teaching and the Brain* and *Grading for Equity*—we have devoted our professional development time to collaboration and discussion, we have brought in outside speakers and supported internal professional learning, and we have invested in pull-out days to provide time for educators to engage.[5] The point being that we have invested time for and provided consistent messaging on this topic. This proactive work helps educators reflect and make positive changes. And while we have made progress, there is still more work to do. It is also possible for situations like the ones described above to occur after you have made progress. Therefore, it is important that we learn to supervise and evaluate effectively so we can respond and continue to help educators grow and improve.

If we were to look at our progress over the first few years of this work, it would probably seem like a bunch of half-baked initiatives. Working with people is messy, and as school leaders, we are working with a lot of people. We need to be clear about our expectations and be patient with the messiness of change. While some people quickly lean into this work, others resist it. But eventually, with consistent messaging, support, and ongoing professional learning, more people will lean into this work, meaning over time, more and more people will grow and improve. Watching this process of growth is the joy of educational leadership. As expectations become clear, we then need to make sure we are responsive and consistent in supervising the work, as well.

One of the responsibilities of instructional leadership is evaluation. Evaluation can be extremely challenging for an antiracist leader due to external pressures, such as state or district evaluation systems, and also due to internal work with individual educators. For those of us in official administrator roles, supervision and evaluation are necessary evils. And as antiracist leaders, we have a responsibility to address these external and internal pressures so that we can foster antiracist classroom experiences for students. This section provides formal and strategic solutions to the challenges of instructional leadership, particularly for those of us who are responsible for supervision and evaluation in our roles.

---

5 Zaretta Hammond, *Culturally Responsive Teaching and the Brain: Promoting Authentic Engagement and Rigor among Culturally and Linguistically Diverse Students* (Thousand Oaks, CA: Corwin, 2015).

Challenging Conversations

While all school leaders wish they could take the coaching lens when helping teachers grow, the reality is that we can all face complex and difficult relationships with educators. When we utilize an antiracist lens, it is problematic to ignore racist practices even when they appear too difficult to address. When we ignore racist ideas and practices, we engage in passive racism and therefore strengthen systemic racism. It is essential that we dive into this difficult work. Think about the situations described in the previous section. How do we address them? How do we make sure students are supported? How do we reduce the possibility of an educator shutting down?

The Difficult Conversation

Antiracist leaders engage in difficult conversations, particularly when they observe racist ideas and practices being used. *Difficult Conversations: How to Discuss What Matters Most* is the book we recommend the most.[6] Additionally, here are a few tips to keep in mind:

- Get to the point. No small talk or talking about other topics. Often this small talk can make the educator more nervous, not less.
- Be specific about an action and give the educator an opportunity to explain, for example, "I noticed that you were using a slavery simulation where students acted as slaves and masters. What's up with that?"
- Be an active listener. What was the intent?
- Give clear feedback. "I understand that your intent was for students to have fun, but playing slavery is not fun. Especially for the students of color in the class. In fact, it

---

6 Douglas Stone, Bruce Patton, and Sheila Heen, *Difficult Conversations: How to Discuss What Matters Most*, 10th anniversary ed. (New York: Penguin, 2010).

perpetuates racist ideas such as white power and makes a difficult topic seem silly."

- Discuss next steps. "Let's come up with a way you can repair with students. We also need to help you develop a more culturally appropriate activity so that students are engaged in this topic."

We have had many difficult conversations in our careers, and believe it or not, most are as straightforward as the example above. Teachers do not enter this profession because they want to do a bad job or hurt kids. But many teachers go years without someone calling them out when they are ineffective, or worse, when they create a culturally insensitive practice. Additionally, most teachers, coming up in this same system, simply did not have an antiracist or diverse education—they cannot pull from their own experience to develop culturally sensitive learning because they have none; they themselves need learning, instruction, and guidance to make this change. Changing the narrative means difficult conversations need to be a part of our practice because they are good for students and educators

Supervising Complicated Personalities

Though most difficult conversations can be straightforward, the reality is that there can be more complicated situations when it comes to supervising educators. Experienced educators who have had very little previous supervision or coaching tend to develop personalities that are challenging to supervise. These educators can be some of the strongest personalities in your school and the most difficult to shift in their practice. Shifting behavior requires strategic action and incorporating the work of other educators. Many educators have experienced failed attempts by previous school leaders. The chart below offers some caricatures of the types of educators that can be challenging to evaluate and strategies you can use to address their practice.

The High-Expectations Colorblind Educator

CHARACTERISTICS: Professes to treat all students the same. Races through their curriculum and expects students to keep up. Relationships must take a back seat.

STRATEGIES: Structure all-staff discussions to share culturally responsive relationship-building activities and explore the benefits of student engagement. Confront lack of interest in relationship building with difficult conversations.

The Go-It-Alone Educator

CHARACTERISTICS: For years, has resisted being told what to do. Opposed to any school or departmental professional development. Pursues their own passions. Fosters strong relationships with students who are similar to them.

STRATEGIES: Often this is the educator who scares administrators (and probably their colleagues) because of their behavior. Confront such behavior in a difficult conversation.

The Stick-to-the-Classics Educator

CHARACTERISTICS: Designs curriculum with a white Eurocentric lens and refers to the materials as "classic." When "forced" to teach about people of color, feels uncomfortable and moves along quickly. Spends lots of time on their own passions.

STRATEGIES: Partner educator in a team with colleagues who are stronger with multicultural lenses. Structure this curricular team to develop common content areas and share best practices.

The Everything-Should-Be-Up-for-Debate Educator

CHARACTERISTICS: Very loose classroom structure. Dives into disagreements among students about every topic without any structure. For example, allows students in a majority-white class to debate whether the N-word should be used when reading a book with racist language.

STRATEGIES: Provide an all-staff meeting on developing classroom agreements when speaking about race. Use the meeting to discuss what debates are off the table, i.e., Holocaust denialism, "slavery was good." In the example given above, forcing students of color who may be offended by white students using the N-word to debate these white students is not safe. Develop a policy with staff about how to address the N-word in literature and primary documents, and how it will be used.

The Caring Teacher with Low Expectations

CHARACTERISTICS: Cares deeply and passionately for students. Makes concessions, e.g., "They must be sleeping in class because they were taking care of their siblings." Students of color receive higher grades in this class than normal. Students of color do not feel connected with this teacher.

STRATEGIES: A difficult conversation about how this perspective lowers expectations and is detrimental for students. Discuss strategies to keep expectations up for students while also demonstrating empathy and scaffolding for the inequitable situations they work within. Work with staff on the "warm demander" concept.

Instructional leadership requires you to engage with educators to support their unique needs. Some educators are motivated and energized to do this work and need coaching. Other educators are more complicated and need more intervention. We cannot just rely on the professional learning structures and ignore how people adapt these ideas in their classroom. Changing the narrative requires being honest and engaging with people. At the same time, we need to recognize people's different levels of racial identity development. As educators work on their own growth in this work, they will develop different needs for support. Where some will take on a lot of responsibility for their own development, others will need connection and sometimes direction.

As discussed before, educators are going to have different levels of experience with talking about race. For example, there may be white educators who have spent very little time considering their privilege and white educators who have a lot of experience teaching with communities of color. Therefore, as you unfold your plan of engagement for staff growth, you will want to provide different on-ramps for support groups. In the same way that wholesale workshops around a topic such as technology do not work for all educators, the same is true for professional development around antiracist practices.

Professional Learning

In this chapter, we have discussed the importance of talking about race, supporting educator growth, and supervision and evaluation. Professional learning is the glue that holds together this work for instructional leaders. This is the work that sets the tone, reduces racist incidents, improves practice, and influences student connection and learning. Professional learning is both proactive and reactive to fostering an antiracist culture. Throughout this section, we provide a frame for incorporating professional learning in your school and note the importance of providing professional learning for all staff in your building.

The Professional Learning Framework

The commitment to antiracist work is ongoing and ever evolving, and strategies will need to be adapted to the specific issue or concern you are trying to address. Educators will want to prioritize strategies that are relevant to their instructional content, the grade level they teach, or their specific roles within your school. Needs will also vary given life experiences and previous exposure to this work. Laying out a vision for the process, inclusive of a learning cycle, will not only help keep your community engaged, but will also help deepen the knowledge and skills needed to make this work effective.

An effective learning cycle for antiracist work should include all members of your school community. Although the majority of your work will be focused on faculty and staff development, engaging students and families in the learning cycle will afford you a more comprehensive approach to addressing the needs for change. The learning cycle should include ongoing exploration that is supplemented with training, assessment, practice, and feedback.

Exploration of self-awareness and racial identity should be a grounding lesson for all involved, but it is not uncommon for faculty and staff to want to skip ahead to training that provides more concrete and strategic approaches in their classrooms. Reassure them that you will get there, but reemphasize the need for this preliminary work to happen first. When introducing this learning cycle to your team, providing a visual of the process can be helpful. Here is an example of a professional learning framework that was developed for a high school community:

1. Self-awareness
2. Personal racial identity development
3. Courageous conversations and skills development
4. Instructional practice and policy change
5. Student and community impact

Furthermore, they use the following actions to monitor and assess:

- Self-reflection: Where am I as it relates to this stage in the work? How am I feeling about the work (e.g., uncomfortable, engaged)? What questions do I have?
- Connections: How can I/we build connections to my/our work? Who are my thought partners? How are we building partnerships with stakeholders and the larger community?
- Skill building: What skills are we identifying as components of growth within the arc? How do these skills play out in practice?
- Growth indicators: What are the measures/indicators of growth?[7]

A framework helps connect the various professional development efforts your school is engaging in. As the work becomes messy and the people lose sight of the purpose, the framework helps you remind them.

Professional Development Examples

Although not exhaustive, we offer several suggestions below for training topics and objectives to engage faculty, students, and families. Before you get to the development and implementation of these workshops, it is important to assess the various learning needs of the members of your school community. Depending on the diversity of roles held in the school, different levels of training may be fitting for those who are in the beginning phases of this work versus those you have identified as members of your leadership team. For those who are at the beginning, you will need to invest time and effort to impart the need for this work and introduce the concepts of racial identity, white privilege, and bias. You and the other leaders in your community will need to reiterate themes in numerous settings. For those who are further along in the journey and have been identified as part of your leadership in this work, training should be modified to include strategic planning and implementation. These will be your partners in bringing other staff members along when resistance occurs.

---

7 Adapted from the Newton South High School Human Rights Council.

Cultural humility

We have previously defined racial identity and white privilege, but what is cultural humility? Often used interchangeably with cultural competence and cultural proficiency, *cultural humility* has become our preferred term in leading antiracist training. Coined by physicians Melanie Tervalon and Jann Murray-Garcia, it is defined as "a lifelong process of learning and critical self-reflection with regard to cultural differences."[8] Additionally, three guiding principles to developing cultural humility are: 1) commit to lifelong learning and critical self-reflection, 2) recognize and challenge power imbalances, 3) advocate for institutional accountability/implementation.[9]

This concept is a great starting point for most antiracist training and underscores the ongoing learning component of this philosophy. Training usually includes activities that invite participants to explore the identities that are most relevant to them, their chosen social circles, fears of engagement in this work, and other self-reflective conversations. The goal is to ground the individual in curiosity and empathy, as well as help them identify limitations of their cultural knowledge based on lack of authentic engagement with other cultures, communities, and systems that aren't present in their day-to-day interactions.

LEARN: Provide a clear definition of cultural humility as a process of ongoing self-reflection and self-critique, one that requires a learner's perspective of seeking to understand and that address structural inequalities by engaging and acknowledging the differences of others.

---

8 Melanie Tervalon and Jann Murray-Garcia, "Cultural Humility Versus Cultural Competence: A Critical Distinction in Defining Physician Training Outcomes in Multicultural Education," *Journal of Health Care for the Poor and Underserved* 9, no. 2 (1998): 117–125.

9 Katherine A. Yeager and Susan Bauer-Wu, "Cultural Humility: Essential Foundation for Clinical Researchers, *Applied Nursing Research* 26, no. 4 (2013): 251–256.

REFLECT: Identify your fears of being in a space where you are not represented as part of the dominant culture and reflect on how it may feel for others when this is their daily experience.

ACT: Make a personal plan to step out of your comfort zone to visit new places and explore new ideas outside of your own norms and standards. Learn more about different cultures and perspectives by developing authentic relationships of inquiry, reading books from racially diverse authors, and watching films with racially diverse characters.

Racial identity development models

Learning about racial identity development (RID) in general, and reflecting on their own racial identity in particular, can help white educators work more effectively with students of color. The white racial identity development model was initially developed by psychologist and educator Janet Helms and has expanded to include additional frameworks by other scholars for multiple racial and ethnic identities.[10]

Racial identity frameworks and models can serve as "tools for self-reflection, for building empathy and understanding of students who are situated differently from yourself, and for transforming your classroom or library into settings that support the positive racial identity of youth of color and Native youth."[11] Many white adults who live and work in predominantly white environments have given little consideration to the meaning of their own racial group membership. The fact that adolescents of color and white youth, along with many white adults, are on very different developmental timelines in terms of racial

---

10 Janet E. Helms, "An Update of Helms's White and People of Color Racial Identity Models," in *Handbook of Multicultural Counseling*, ed. Joseph G. Ponterotto et al. (Thousand Oaks, CA: Sage, 1995), 181–198. Also go to HenryJTurner.com/ChangeTheNarrative for racial identity models.

11 "Summary of Racial and Ethnic Identity Frameworks or Models," Project READY, January 2019, ready.web.unc.edu/wp-content/uploads/sites/16627/2019/01/SUMMARY-OF-RACIAL-AN D-ETHNIC-IDENTITY-MODELS.pdf.

identity is often a source of misunderstanding and potential conflict.[12] Training in RID models should include opportunities to explore critical developmental moments, such as the first time they discovered race and stages/moments in life where perspectives changed or were reaffirmed, e.g., going to college, moving to a new city/town, international travel, etc. Providing opportunities to make connections to the impact these moments had and the messages they carried can help provide more context for recognizing how significant a role race places in a person's life and choices.

LEARN: Consider how the context of an individual's life will affect their racial and ethnic identity development and have an impact on positive or neutral attitudes and identities they may form. Connect this to how one shows up in their personal and professional community, including in a school environment and in relationships with students and family members.

REFLECT: Think about the first time you discovered race. What was the positive or negative message you took away about your racial group and other racial groups? What events in life caused you to think about or change your views on race? How does this show up in your relationships with colleagues and students?

ACT: Choose the developmental stage you most identify with and reflect on the key moments that led you there. Then choose the stage you would like to move to next and develop a personal plan for how you will expand your learning to reach it.

Introducing culturally responsive instruction

As described earlier in this chapter, educators may struggle with implementing this practice in the classroom. You can use this framework in workshops and training to develop concrete strategies that

12 Beverly Daniel Tatum, *Why Are All the Black Kids Sitting Together in the Cafeteria?: And Other Conversations about Race* (New York: Basic Books, 2017).

offer a diversity of cultures and ideas. These strategies are grounded in providing rigorous, personalized instruction that connects academic concepts to students' lived experiences. Teachers will also learn the value of building cultural and sociopolitical awareness to connect with students and access their highest potential.

> **LEARN:** Engage the audience in thinking about their own practices and provide strategies to incorporate culturally responsive approaches in the classroom that will invite and engage all students into their learning environment by honoring the legitimacy of different cultures, teaching to the "whole child," and treating the classroom like a community.
>
> **REFLECT:** Are there activities or classroom norms that unintentionally exclude students from participating? Are your curricula, content, and celebrations representative of ALL students in the classroom and school population?
>
> **ACT:** Create opportunities to invite student stories and individual cultures into the classroom by pronouncing names correctly. Communicate high expectations and disrupt traditional norms that may exclude certain students. Lead with exploration and minimize assumptions about student performance and participation.

Creating a welcoming environment for students and families

This presentation explores the social-emotional impact of unconscious biases on youth, families, and their engagement and feelings of belonging in education. The presentation can incorporate personal reflections, data, and interactive discussion to examine individual and group biases, as well as develop applicable strategies to engage the community in conversations and activities that promote inclusion.

LEARN: Develop strategies to engage key members of your school community to assess the current culture and climate, and identify structures and practices that may exclude certain students and family members. The goal is to identify tools and develop strategies that can be applied in classrooms, programs, and the overall school community to promote a welcoming environment that is representative and inclusive of all members.

REFLECT: How do decisions impact students/families and their feelings of belonging? How does this impact your relationships with students? With parents? What opportunities are you creating to be open?

ACT: Be mindful of the privilege you may hold in different situations, such as profession, gender, or class. Create opportunities to learn more about the needs of your students and their family. Collectively design a space that is reflective of the community's diversity, e.g., culture, physical ability, learning style, etc.

Workshop for counselors, social workers, and support staff

This training provides a learning experience for counselors, social workers, and other support staff in a process of self-reflection and self-critique on issues of diversity and cultural humility in their relationships with students. Participants will be guided to build a community of shared goals with their students within the context of their professional relationships as support staff and will learn strategies for how to create welcoming and inclusive messages in their counseling space, better initiate and support conversations about difference (race, gender, power, etc.), acknowledge relevant social issues, and reinforce trust and emotional safety to help students feel more connected to the counseling process.

LEARN: Get comfortable and strategic in acknowledging the power dynamics (e.g., age, race, gender, etc.) in your counseling relationships in order to create a safe space for students to be authentic in sharing their experiences.

REFLECT: How does your counseling space convey that all students with diverse identities are welcome? How comfortable are you in asking questions about race, culture, and identity and including it as part of your practice?

ACT: Ask students to list the three most important things about their culture. Use this information to connect to how they are sharing their experiences in school and in their relationships with classmates and teachers.

Culture in sports and coaching

Racism, sexism, and homophobia still make their way into locker rooms, practices, games, and bus rides. Too often, incidents go unreported or overlooked out of fear of backlash for speaking up, whether for yourself or for others.

In this workshop, coaches and student athletes will learn more about harmful sports culture and its negative impact on players and teams. They will discuss tools and strategies to help them feel more confident in speaking up for themselves and as an ally, and learn what it means to be an upstander, rather than a bystander.

LEARN: Unpack a history of harmful sports culture that includes racism, sexism, homophobia, cultural appropriation, and aggressive coaching tactics to better understand the negative impact on young players and team behaviors, particularly for those who are members of marginalized groups.

> **REFLECT:** Think about decisions you have made and/or overlooked as a coach that may have excluded members of marginalized groups (because of race, gender, sexual orientation, etc.) and impacted their feelings of belonging and safety.
>
> **ACT:** Develop a feedback process to learn more about the experiences of your athletes with the goal of creating more inclusive team dynamics and fostering emotional and physical safety.

Conclusion

At a foundational level, learning and teaching are the purpose of schools. While the antiracist leadership framework shows different facets of our work, what happens in the classroom cannot be ignored. At the same time, shifting classroom practices can be complicated and challenging. This work requires clear professional development and instructional leadership. This leadership needs to be focused on antiracism and culturally responsive instructional practices, but it also requires leaders who can effectively challenge educators, whether through coaching or having difficult conversations. We cannot move our schools forward if we ignore this work.

Developing a professional learning plan is vital to ensuring there is a common understanding of what antiracism is and looks like in your school community. It also encourages mutual investment from all stakeholders. Given the diversity of needs and varying levels of previous training in this work, it will also require offering a variety of options and reaffirming that the cycle is ongoing and never fully complete.

Most importantly, in order to engage members to their full capacity, creating safe spaces for growth and learning is imperative. This not only requires agreed-upon norms and standards, but also holding participants accountable when an agreement is violated and harm is inflicted. Be mindful of microaggressions that may be directed toward your communities of color and create restorative opportunities when possible.

KEY IDEAS

- Race and racism have to be at the center of your work and consistently incorporated into instructional supervision. Educators need to learn about their own racial identity and focus on their development.
- Instructional leadership must also be learner centered. Effective leaders are able to include coaching strategies that help teachers learn and grow in this work.
- Culturally responsive instruction is an antiracist and student-centered approach for all educators to learn and adapt to their instructional strategies.
- Antiracist leaders are also effective at developing and adjusting strategies to work with resistant and complicated teachers.
- Professional development can be adapted to address the various skills and needs of your learning community. Constantly assess learning needs to respond with effective training and supervision opportunities.

CHANGE THE NARRATIVE

LEARN-Read Zaretta Hammond's *Culturally Responsive Teaching and the Brain*.

REFLECT-Watch Jamila Lyiscott's TED Talk "3 Ways to Speak English."[13] Journal about how her lens of being trilingual connects with your understanding of learning.

---

13 Jamila Lyiscott. "3 Ways to Speak English." TED Talk. TED Salon NY2014, February 2014. ted.com/talks/jamila_lyiscott_3_ways_to_speak_english.

ACT-Practice having different kinds of difficult conversations with other school leaders. Set a goal to have more difficult conversations when you discover ineffective practice.

ASSESS-Use the Learning for Justice Social Justice Standards to assess which classrooms and curricular areas students learn these skills in and which they do not.

CHAPTER 9

THE ANTIRACIST STUDENT EXPERIENCE

Children learn more from what you are than what you teach.

—W. E. B. DU BOIS

School is one of the most influential places in our lives when it comes to our racial identity development. It is where we spend the majority of our childhood and is a central place where messages of success, work ethic, and power are reinforced. Often BIPOC students do not see themselves in this narrative. This is why it is of the utmost importance to consider how the messages coming from your school community may exclude different cultures and identities, leaving some to feel inferior, unseen, and inadequate.

For many white students, learning history from a Eurocentric perspective, reading books written by white authors, being educated by white teachers, and being in classrooms with other white students reinforces a resounding message that they are "normal" and "standard." Students of color, who are consuming the same materials in the same classrooms, receive the same messages about the dominance of white culture and are left to feel "different" and "substandard."

As students of color in majority-white schools, both of us experienced this message. Our school experience often found us the only students of color in our classrooms and on our sports teams, and we rarely (if ever) saw teachers that resembled our complexion. And though we are successful in our careers despite this reality, it is also clear that this dynamic pushes more BIPOC students down than it allows to thrive.

Being an antiracist leader means that you are committed and willing to decenter the culture of whiteness and to create a school environment that supports and empowers ALL students to feel safe, welcomed, and efficacious in their learning community. You are tasked with providing opportunities for students to learn about the history and impact of racism, to support educators as they shift practices to include conversations about race and difference, and to provide opportunities for students to feel empowered in their own advocacy about things that matter to them. This chapter will help you think about how to structure these pieces for your student community.

Student Learning

We spend a considerable amount of time in this book highlighting and supporting the need for your own learning as a leader, as well as for designing opportunities for educators and communities to invest in their own learning. This process will not be complete or comprehensive if we do not include our major stakeholders—the students—in a parallel process. In fact, much of our learning about race as adults is actually the practice of unlearning what we consumed in our formative years, some of which was introduced through our formal education. Investing in student learning in pre-K to 12 helps students build a healthy understanding and ability to have conversations about race and difference as they progress in their formal education. This includes creating space for this learning in classrooms and supporting your educators to prepare safe spaces for this to take place.

A common argument in resistance to this work is that children are too young to have conversations about race, but research shows this generalization is inaccurate. Infants notice differences in the melanin content of people's skin and begin developing prejudiced ideas about race as early as age two.[1] Children can begin critically engaging in these conversations at age five, with thoughtful reflection, ideas, and questions.[2] At the same time children's self-perceptions are shaped by others, such as parents and family members, but also by teachers and classmates, as well. Just like adults, young children can internalize stereotypes and form negative opinions about who they are if we do not give them the words to unpack their feelings and experiences. We must build their capacity to develop counternarratives to refute these damaging beliefs.[3]

Another common misbelief is that predominantly white schools do not need to learn about or invest in conversations about race because their student body is not diverse. This is based on the problematic assumption that learning about race and the impact of racism is only necessary when people of color are present. This thinking is centered in whiteness and privilege and relieves white people from the responsibility of having conversations or learning about others' experiences and stories. It further creates a pattern of disconnect and lack of understanding about how to engage with others who are different when they step outside their comfort zone of homogeneity. To believe that unpacking race and racism is not necessary for communities who do not interact with different races only reinforces the ignorance and misinformation that keep racist practices and systems alive. In fact, predominantly white communities need this work *more* than others because it will better prepare students to engage in conversations about race as they transition into adulthood.

Student learning is an essential component of your antiracist commitment, and there are several ways it can be formally and informally

---

1 Sandy Sangrigoli and Scania de Schonen, "Recognition of Own-Race and Other-Race Faces by Three-Month-Old Infants," *Journal of Child Psychology and Psychiatry* 45, no. 7 (2004): 1219–1227; Lawrence A. Hirschfeld, "Children's Developing Conceptions of Race," in *The Handbook of Race, Racism, and the Developing Child*, eds. Stephen M. Quintana and Clark McKown (Hoboken, NJ: Wiley, 2008), 37–54.

2 Po Bronson and Ashley Merryman, *NurtureShock: New Thinking about Children* (New York: Twelve, 2009).

3 Louise Derman-Sparks and Julie Olsen Edwards, *Anti-Bias Education for Young Children and Ourselves*, (Washington, DC: NAEYC Books, 2010).

embedded into your classrooms and larger school community, through activities, clubs, sports, etc. Below are a few ideas and key areas that move beyond singular classroom projects or activities to create opportunities for you to invite students to engage with their understanding of race and their own racial identities.

Foundations of Race

Within the racial identity model, we learn that messages about race present themselves as early as preschool. Engaging students in the history of the concept of race, identifying messages within the media, and learning about the harmful impact of stereotypes can never begin too early. This workshop can use storytelling, media clips, and research on the history of race in America to engage students in their own connection to values and identity. It will encourage them to learn about different cultures, ask thoughtful questions, and become more comfortable discussing race and unpacking their stories, biases, and questions in order to dismantle some of the harmful thoughts and behaviors students experience.

LEARN: Introduce and discuss the concept of race to provide a foundation for students to develop an informed and factual understanding of how race was socially constructed to intentionally enforce a system of hierarchy and classification.

REFLECT: Discuss the following questions: When was the first time race was formally introduced to you in a learning environment? What misconceptions did you have that were debunked in this learning?

ACT: Use race-friendly books and structured lesson plans to have conversations that deconstruct false narratives and biased thinking about race and embrace learning about difference and diversity as core values in your classroom.

Upstander vs. Bystander

Most likely upon reflection, we can all recall moments in school when we either were not the best version of ourselves or witnessed (or participated in) interactions that now make us cringe. As educators, we cannot anticipate every moment and also do not have a blueprint for how to resolve every student conflict seamlessly. What we have learned is that we must get involved with student conflict, even when it is complicated. And this is the message we want to impart to our students about recognizing harm and building skills to stand up for themselves and for others.

This is the role of an upstander: "a person who speaks or acts in support of an individual or cause, particularly someone who intervenes on behalf of a person being attacked or bullied."[4] Students are frequently exposed to harmful behaviors and acts of racism throughout their education in classrooms, sports teams, clubs, and friendship circles. Like adults, students may default to passive racism—they hear things that they inherently know are not right, participate in banter and behaviors they may not agree with, and overlook harmful acts to others because they feel powerless or afraid. By being a bystander, they reinforce the impact of the harm. In the workshop below, students can discuss tools and strategies to help them feel more confident in speaking up as an ally, and learn what it means to be an upstander, rather than a bystander.

> **LEARN:** Discuss the unintended impact of racist language, behavior, and practices. Additionally, support students as they learn what it means to become an ally and upstander, rather than a bystander.

---

4 "Upstander," Facing History & Ourselves, updated October 19, 2021, facinghistory.org/upstander.

REFLECT: Think about a time you witnessed a racist interaction with a friend, colleague, student, or even stranger. Did you intervene? If not, what fears kept you from speaking up? How could your interference have supported the person who was being harmed?

ACT: Ask students to share ideas and strategies that help them feel more confident in speaking up as an ally and to identify a trusting adult in the school community they can go to when they witness bullying or racist words or actions. Encourage the informal and formal leaders in your class, groups, clubs, or sports to be a leaders for all students.

In many of our investigations of racial incidents that happen in the classroom, on social media, or during an extracurricular activity, we find that students who were witnesses to the event knew that the offending words or actions were harmful. Yet they did little to intervene, or sometimes even went along with it. Some of this is due to the developmental nature of children and adolescents—though adults are no less guilty of standing passively in an effort to avoid conflict. But we have also discovered that their silence may be the result of not knowing what to say in the moment. Being a bystander and ignoring or avoiding racial incidents only perpetuates the acceptance of a dominant standard of racism and works to protect the person who inflicts harm rather than the victim. Teaching children about actions that can break this cycle and support their being an ally and upstander not only supports antiracist work, but is also in line with the goal of helping students grow up to be good citizens.

Students should be encouraged to stand up for their friends and classmates of color and to identify trusted adults in the building to whom they can report any racial incidents they witness. As adults, we should reinforce this behavior with our own modeling, but also support and commend students who take risks as courageous leaders.

Below are some tips educators can share with students on the differences between being a bystander and an upstander.

Bystander versus Upstander

Bystander

- Doesn't say anything, even if they know it's wrong
- Laughs along because others are
- Thinks it has nothing to do with them, so they shouldn't intervene
- Tells the victim not to make it a big deal

Upstander

- Doesn't join in on the jokes
- Says something in the moment
- Supports the victim—shows concern and asks how to help
- Tells a trusted adult
- Mobilizes others to stand up and speak out

What We Should Expect in the Classroom

Students spend the majority of their school time in classrooms. Therefore, it is important to ensure that all classrooms have a similar focus so that students of color are welcomed, supported, and have an opportunity to excel in these spaces. Additionally, when students of color are absent from these classrooms, it is essential that antiracist school cultures maintain a focus on empowering the voices of people of color and other marginalized students.

Social and Emotional Development

We have learned that facilitating conversations and lessons about race can be daunting for both educators and students, but if time and energy are spent up front on creating a classroom community that prioritizes social and emotional learning and values all students as a part of the community, then a stronger foundation will exist when difficult moments arise.

Creating safety in the classroom does not happen overnight and should be a part of the culture of an educator's class from the first day of school. Begin by setting up your classroom so it is representative of a diversity of cultures and identities, with images, books, quotes, languages, celebrations, toys, and lessons. Continue to build on this as the school year progresses and invite input from your students to add to and expand representation in the classroom. Make sure to learn and correctly pronounce your students' names. This may seem like a small gesture, but we carry our identities in our names and mispronouncing or shortening someone's name repeatedly can unintentionally send a message that they do not belong. In fact, the easiest change we made in our school was to create columns in our student information system that allows students to write their name phonetically and list their preferred name and preferred pronouns.

Invite students to share about themselves and what is important to them in their learning. This can be done with a classroom activity or by having students write their thoughts down privately. Learning about your students allows you to individualize your lesson plans to be more inclusive and accessible to different learning needs. Taking the time to set up your classroom community will help students feel they belong, creating a foundation of trust and respect for more difficult topics regarding race and identity.

Classroom Agreements List

Creating a list of classroom agreements is a consistent way to set expectations and structure in your classroom.[5] Many teachers may have a set of standards they share every year that includes words like "respect" and "treat others how you would like to be treated." Enhance your standards by offering students the opportunity to add to the list to

---

5 We prefer the term *agreement* over *norm*.

create a shared understanding of what respect in the classroom looks like to them. We strongly advise having a list of agreements visible and accessible in your classroom while ensuring you always hold each and every student accountable when a norm or agreement is breached. The consistency and equity in this practice will build trust that all students are treated fairly and that no one student is above accountability or consequence.

Oftentimes classroom rules are heavily focused on compliance and social restraints, e.g., "stay in your seat," "keep your hands to yourself," "remove your hat," etc. While it is understandable that some level of consistency and structure should be reinforced in a classroom with multiple student learners, it is just as important to create agreements guided by shared values and emotional safety and that support differentiated learning. Agreements can be introduced by the classroom teacher but should also invite input from students and ultimately be agreed upon by the class community to increase buy-in and honor individualism and inclusion.

Below are a few agreements to consider introducing to your students, while asking them to add to the list, as well:

Sample Classroom Agreements

- Use preferred names and pronouns.
- Be respectful of yourself and others.
- Make a commitment to learning and understanding.
- Be open-minded to different ideas and opinions.
- Ask questions if/when unsure.
- Be mindful of including others.
- Try on new ways of thinking.
- Support each other's learning.

A Classroom Culture Celebrates Its Diversity

To be prepared for these conversations, you must also recognize and acknowledge the racialized context that exists in your classroom and school community and how it may impact students of color or members of marginalized groups every day. Children can become privy to what is happening around them via media and social media, and also through adults and other children. Depending on their developmental stage, they may not understand all of the details and contexts, but they can discern a general sentiment of fear, anger, or discomfort at the world around them. Furthermore, people often suggest that children should be shielded from the harsh realities of our world, that they are precious and innocent, but this reflects a very significant privilege. Which children get to be saved from the realities of poverty, war, crime, and environmental catastrophe, and which children face these realities in their own lives? Avoiding topics or wishing them away does not honor the experiences of students who live through these realities, and in fact it may further disempower them and heighten their sense of isolation and invisibility.

The COVID-19 pandemic offers a telling example of this in the disproportionate health and financial consequences communities of color have suffered compared to their white counterparts.[6] Having this information informs educators of a potential disparity in their students' experiences of illness, grief, and loss, as well as access to resources such as housing and health care. Taking this into consideration can then help you support students who may appear to be disengaged by inviting them to share what would be helpful and supportive rather than penalizing them. Take time to learn your students' stories and about where they are coming from to build on an antiracist learning environment that acknowledges how personal stories and experiences impact student learning.

---

6 "Health Equity Considerations and Racial and Ethnic Minority Groups," Centers for Disease Control and Prevention, updated January 25, 2022, cdc.gov/coronavirus/2019-ncov/community/health-equity/race-ethnicity.html.

Setting up Your Classroom for Success

- Set up a welcoming space.
- Invest in relationships.
- Learn names and their correct pronunciation.
- Create classroom agreements together.
- Understand racialized context; don't wish it away.
- Explore, don't assume.
- Provide options to engage.
- Ask what they need.

Conversations and Lessons on Race

Like most classroom lessons, discussion works best when there is clarity in the purpose of the conversation and transparency about the intended goal. When addressing a specific topic or introducing a lesson that is centered on race, be clear of the purpose of the lesson and the plan for the day and be specific about agreements. Having a template for the lesson will help ground the conversation and allow you to redirect when questions or comments begin to veer in a different direction. Provide a list of basic agreements for the conversation and commit to holding students accountable throughout the lesson or conversation. Also open up suggestions for students to add what they believe will be necessary for them to feel safe in the discussion.

Below is a sample guide for educators who want to address a topic in class, either in response to a racist event or to present concepts. Once you've decided to address a topic in class, create a plan to introduce it.

Facilitator Discussion Guide on Race

Preparation:

Determine the specific purpose of the conversation and relay it in developmentally appropriate language. Examples include:

- Acknowledge and process a harmful racist incident that occurred either in the classroom, the school community, or in the wider public.
- Teach a historical narrative that may include violence and harm to a particular racial group.
- Learn, honor, and celebrate a culture that is traditionally underrepresented in our dominant culture.

Write up specific agreements to present prior to the conversation. Examples include:

- Raise your hand and wait to be called on before sharing.
- Do not interrupt others when they are speaking.
- Speak from "I" statements only.
- Do not dismiss anyone's experience, but ask to learn more.

Before and During:

- Present the purpose and answer any clarifying questions.
- Go over agreements and open it up to students to add additional items that would help secure safety.
- Provide options for those who are uncomfortable or prefer to process in another space.

Closing:

- Thank the class for their respectful and thoughtful participation.
- Check in by having students share one word about how they feel the discussion went.

> - Acknowledge that this may not have resolved the issue, but it's important to give it space.
> - Brainstorm ideas for follow up, if necessary.
> - Offer options for students who need to process more, such as a counselor, social worker, or trusted adult.

Students Need to See Themselves in the Curriculum

From our experience working in schools, there are three kinds of experiences for students in a classroom when it comes to racial diversity within curriculum:

1. *"Whites only"*—In these classrooms, the curriculum is focused solely on the perspective of white Americans. BIPOC figures play a subservient role or are secondary players to the story. Examples of this include an English curriculum focused on the "classics," a world history curriculum focused on Europe; a math or science class that professes to be colorblind; a world language class that is focused only on the European culture of the language and ignores non-European cultures.

2. *Add-on*—These classrooms are still very much focused on white-dominant curricula but include the stories of people of color at select times during the year. A teacher may, for example, discuss Black history in February during Black History Month; or an English teacher may select a book by a person of color.

3. *Inclusive and representative*—These classrooms start with the premise that there is no one dominant culture and include the stories of diverse peoples. They make sure the voices of people of color are heard and ensure a diverse range of protagonists. This may look like a history curriculum that accepts as a starting point that there is a great diversity of human culture; a math and science curriculum that accepts cultural representation as

a foundational goal; or a world language curriculum that starts with the diaspora of language.

Students of color rarely see themselves in a curriculum, and when they do, they are often portrayed as savages or victims. Furthermore, when these topics are brought up in many classrooms, teachers are underprepared to talk about racial history. It is important again to remind ourselves that teachers have emerged from the same educational and broader social system that is now being challenged—in other words, many teachers did not necessarily learn this history themselves—and now they are expected to be able to teach students something different.

Henry remembers taking a US history class in middle school and being the only Black student in the class. One time he was disciplined and sent to the back of the classroom for talking during class. Moments later, as the class was covering the Montgomery bus boycotts, the teacher stopped the class and called out, "Henry, I'm just realizing that I sent you to the back of the bus like Rosa Parks. I'm sorry. Come to the front of the class." Henry stood up and walked to the front of the class as the rest of the class laughed at him. Not only was the teacher underprepared to talk about the topic, he was underprepared to talk about race. While this story was over thirty years ago, unfortunately it could still happen today.

To create a culturally relevant curriculum, teachers need to value inclusivity and build their curriculum based on that value. Here are some strategies to move toward an inclusive and representative curriculum:

- Start with a vision and goals that are focused on representation.
- Be comfortable with complex narratives. When we focus on "clean" narratives we are most likely going to create a whitewashed version.
- Ask students of color how they feel about the curriculum you are currently using. Where do they see themselves in it? Are there topics they feel are overtold or under-told?

A final consideration for your inclusive and representative curriculum is to be clear on the skills students are expected to develop. Teachers should consider helping students develop such skills in their curriculum. To do this, courses need to start with a student-centered approach that empowers students to be engaged and solve problems. As we suggested before, consider using Learning for Justice Social Justice Standards and focus on skill development.

Empower

As students get older and transition out of elementary school, they become more curious about current events. Additionally, with the spike in social media over the last few decades, it is almost impossible to avoid issues of race. We see schools as a prime place to encourage students to develop their own voices and become advocates in the things that matter to them.

Supporting Social Justice Leaders

Offering electives or clubs that speak to social justice issues can provide space for students who want to be with other like-minded students, as well as learn more about topics they feel connected to. Leadership in a Diverse Society is a course we offer in our school to juniors and seniors who have been nominated, either by a teacher or classmate, as someone who has demonstrated leadership in the school community. Throughout the course, topics about various identities, inclusive of race, gender, and class are presented and dissected with an emphasis on narratives, articles, images, guest speakers, and classroom discussion to go deep into unpacking our biases, stereotypes, and misunderstandings.

Students are encouraged to think about social justice issues and take initiative to create change in their school community. As you may remember, Henry met with the students in this course after the Confederate flag incident. These students also responded to later racist incidents in the school, developed a list of demands for students of color, and facilitated student-led vigils after horrific events. This course serves as a catalyst not only to equip students with the knowledge and self-discovery necessary to be an antiracist leader, but also to empower them to stand firm in their values as they discover their own way of contributing to a broader society. Without fail, every year students reflect on their personal growth and develop a deeper understanding of different perspectives. Often, they inquire why this course is not mandated for all students. In 2020, we made progress with that by creating an English course called Action through Literature, which allows more students to develop these skills.

Student empowerment does not need to be formal, either. For example, when a student approached Henry about developing a program of speakers to discuss the Holocaust with students, he connected her with a teacher who could help make it happen. Not only did other students benefit from the program, but the student organizer also learned how she could create change in her school and community. The important message is that we provide space and time for students to create change.

Conclusion

As leaders, building an antiracist school community is centered on providing an educational experience for students in which they feel safe enough to fully engage in their own learning and expand the possibilities available to them. Acknowledging race and identity in the classroom is not only encouraged, it is necessary to ensure all students can show up as themselves, in the identities that are present and non-negotiable to them. This requires a shift in our educational curriculum and practices, and it requires all educators to invite voices into the classroom that are frequently left out and to design opportunities for these voices to be empowered and active alongside the work of their teachers, principals, and administration.

This chapter outlined specific areas to consider in thinking about the student experience, beginning in the classroom and expanding to the broader school community. Not all of these actions can be taken at once, but they can be added and built on over time. Listening and responding to students' needs and supporting their skill building in conversations about race, difference, and identity will help empower them to take the lead on creating the community they want.

KEY IDEAS

- Relationships are essential to creating a learning environment in which students feel safe to discuss issues of race. Be curious and invite stories to learn more about your students and their experiences.
- Partner with your students to create norms and agreements to guide your conversations about race. Hold one another accountable when agreements are broken. This will enhance trust and safety.
- Create opportunities for students to engage in advocacy that is aligned with their interests, values and skills.

CHANGE THE NARRATIVE

LEARN–Design an age-appropriate activity to learn more about your students. Include questions that will solicit information about their culture, values, interests and fears. Assess the activity for safety and inclusion.

REFLECT–Think back to when you were a student and ask yourself what you wished your teachers knew about you back then. Use this reflection to be creative in engaging your students to share more.

ACT–Review your school activities and classroom lessons with an antiracist lens to remove narratives or practices that are harmful or project a white-dominant focus. Include materials and topics that are representative of a diversity of cultures and practices and invite students to process what they have learned and raise any questions they have.

ASSESS-Provide options for student feedback (public and anonymous) following discussions, curriculum, or incidents involving race.

CHAPTER 10

DISMANTLING RACIST POLICIES AND STRUCTURES

Some rules are nothing but old habits that people are afraid to change.

—THERESE ANNE FOWLER

It has been said that high schools are slow to grow and evolve. In fact, a common critique is that the typical high school structure has not changed since it was developed at the turn of the twentieth century.[1] And while the criticism exists and is warranted, we can hear in the school hallway: "If it ain't broke, don't fix it." But given what we know about marginalized communities' experiences of school—with high dropout and discipline rates, oversized and underfunded classrooms, etc.—can we confidently say that schools are not broken? And if school is not broken, who are our schools working for?

Schools were built around an industrial model designed to teach children how to take orders, how to obey authority, how to sit still for the duration of the workday—in short, it teaches children about their position within a hierarchy and power relationships. High schools were designed to separate the students who were preparing for college from those who were destined to become laborers. It is also important

---

1 David B. Tyack and Larry Cuban, *Tinkering toward Utopia: A Century of Public School Reform*, (Cambridge, MA: Harvard University Press, 1995).

to remember that this structure through most of the twentieth century was only for white students, with Black students attending separate and unfunded schools. Still, the structure remains.

While we may have softened the language for how we separate students, too often our schools continue to build on the foundation of separation. When we do not question systems, we allow our bias to be baked into them, and therefore allow the marginalization and racism within these systems and policies to continue. It is common to hear a defense of the policies and structures of our schools as if they were created based on sound research, instead of a culture that prioritized separation. Through education dog whistles, such as "These students can't handle heterogeneous classes" and "Suspension is the proper way to send a message when students misbehave," a culture of dominance persists. This mindset prevents any change from occurring.

Many of these policies and structures that we defend, such as grading and discipline, demonstrate disparities between students of color and white students. As described in chapter 1, BIPOC students are the most disciplined, have higher rates of special education services, and receive lower grades. We hide behind these policies and then wonder what the solution is. The policy *is* the problem. We give students double math when their grades are too low, we develop behavior plans when they are disciplined, and we overidentify students of color as disabled when they struggle behaviorally and academically. How often do we look at our system, our practices, or our policies as the problem?

Too often, we look at individual cases to justify our decisions and wonder why we struggle to reduce these racial disparities. While this book has focused largely on the work of the leader in fostering an antiracist culture, the reality is that our practices and culture are not going to shift until we dismantle existing policies and create antiracist policies that are focused on the concepts of learning. Through new policies, we can create schools that are built on love, equity, and learning for all students. Still, we have to do the work we've discussed in order to create antiracist policies.

Our schools and policies emerge from a racist, top-down perspective, and we need to be collaborative, thoughtful, deliberate, and strategic in how we dismantle these policies so that new policies are not founded on the same racist ideas, further hurting students. Built on the framework of strategic action described and expanded upon in previous chapters, the purpose of this chapter is to help leaders identify racist policies, understand the timing for when to dismantle a policy strategically and effectively, and take steps to dismantle the policy and develop a more antiracist one. It is essential to follow the learning cycle model and make sure each step is deliberate. Finally, we use examples of existing policies to evaluate how they could be made more antiracist. We recognize that there are many unique policies in each school that need to be evaluated and dismantled if we are to change the narrative. We hope these examples will help you to think about strategies to use in your school.

How to Dismantle Existing Policies

When we think of school policies, we should keep in mind Ibram Kendi's observation that "racist policies are founded upon racist ideas."[2] As explained, the structure of school has not changed in more than a hundred years and was built on sorting students for either college or the workforce during a time of de jure and de facto segregation throughout the United States. Considering these origins, it is fair to accept that many of our school policies were founded upon racist ideas.

These policies have been unchanged for so long, they feel like institutions in themselves, and they feel unchangeable. We are familiar with one school district that was eliminating weighted GPA on the transcript as a measure of reducing stress in the school. Community members filled the auditorium during a School Committee meeting to argue that the school system was ruining their children's chances to go to college. As is often the case, the argument against the change

---

2 Ibram X. Kendi, *How to Be an Antiracist* (New York: One World, 2019), 18.

was layered with fear that elitism and tradition were being erased. When the path—which is clear for some students who want to get into a competitive college—is changed, educators are accused of hurting the school's reputation. The false argument that the path is unimpeded and open to any student who simply works hard ignores the tutors, college coaches, test-prep coaches, and many other supports that some of the most privileged students receive and, in many ways, distracts from what should be the purpose of school—learning.

As we make strides to increase the number of students prepared for the postsecondary world, gaps remain between white and Asian students and Black, Latinx, and Indigenous students. We have to uncover the roots of our cultural beliefs in certain policies and understand the impact they have on students. Research regularly identifies low grades as a precursor for students dropping out.[3] But while we add more supports, such as flexible learning time and innovative strategies to help struggling students improve, we must consider the policy as the problem.

No matter the intention, top-down decision making is not the solution to changing these policies. Changing policy in this manner reinforces the very inequitable structures we are trying to dismantle. Rather, policy making must be inclusive in the same manner as are other aspects of developing an antiracist culture. As leaders, we must push the community to engage in the difficult conversation around these structures and systems, even when the majority is in favor of staying the course. Our leadership must be driven by data and research to help our communities understand how a policy can hurt students and why more equitable policies are good for all students. This section focuses on the steps to take to dismantle racist policies in your school.

---

3 "Early Warning Indicators," in *High School Dropout, Graduation, and Completion Rates: Better Data, Better Measures, Better Decisions*, National Research Council, eds. Robert M. Hauser and Judith Anderson Koenig (Washington, DC: National Academies Press, 2011), 61–71, nap.edu/read/13035/chapter/7.

Setting a New Vision through Policy Making

School policies and systems reinforce the values of the school. Therefore, if we create values based around equity, how can we not change our policies? As Bettina Love wrote, school should be about "LOVE."[4] Similarly, our policies should be driven by love instead of a desire to separate and punish students. It is only when students who feel the most disconnected from our schools feel loved by their school that they will engage, take risks with us, thrive, and ultimately learn. Doing this means developing ever-evolving policies based on the needs of our students and the progression of our learning.

Schools based on love set clear policy visions for what they want school to look like so that students can thrive. They understand that these policy changes will push all educators to shift their practices to reach this vision.

WHAT ANTIRACIST SCHOOLS DO	WHAT ANTIRACIST SCHOOLS DO NOT DO
Give students feedback on their progress	Sort and rank students for postsecondary demands
Restorative practices focused on learning and repair	Punish students
Assess in multiple ways what students know and can do	High-stakes testing
Value diverse students learning together	Track students
Empower students	Disempower students
Hire and retain educators who represent the student body	Colorblind hiring policies

---

4 Bettina L. Love, *We Want to Do More than Survive: Abolitionist Teaching and the Pursuit of Educational Freedom* (Boston: Beacon Press, 2019).

The table above outlines some of the policy changes we have prioritized in our work. We do not pretend this is an exhaustive list, but it helps push our thinking about how we can create a new antiracist policy.

Creating Antiracist Policies

Using the learn-reflect-act-assess learning cycle of inquiry can provide a thoughtful and deliberate process for our policy changes, ensuring those changes are focused on efficacy and student need.

Cycle of Inquiry for Policy Change

Learn about the inequity that exists within a policy. How is the policy creating inequity for students of color? What is the historic rationale for the policy? What data demonstrates racial inequity? Does the policy disproportionately advantage white students or other privileged groups? Does the policy seek to separate students or does it focus on learning?

Reflect on the implications of changing the policy. How could the policy adhere more closely to the school's focus on learning and not separating students?

Act on informed and transparent change. Did you communicate the racist nature of the policy and how the change is going to address equity concerns?

Assess the impact (positive and negative) the policy is having on students. What further changes (additional or reverting back) need to occur?

The cycle of inquiry allows leaders to use an informed structure that provides schools the opportunity to continuously evaluate the efficacy of the policy. Leaders should use the same strategies outlined in chapter 4 about how to engage all members of the community on changing the policy. For example, effective policy-making is transparent and utilizes communication strategies to engage community members. Additionally, students should play a role in policy changes so they are not left feeling as though policies are imposed on them. The process for incorporating student voices should ensure that a diverse range of students is heard. As we have shared before, how we communicate and engage with staff, students, and families in this process is critical.

Examples of Antiracist Policy Change

The remainder of this chapter focuses on several policies that we have experience working on. We hope that sharing our experiences will help you to take on some of your own policies. Although some of these policy changes are still in progress, they touch upon some of the most established structures of our school.

School safety

Racial discipline disparities remain a common problem in American schools. BIPOC students are suspended at higher rates than their white counterparts. One study conducted at the secondary level found that discipline caused Black students to lose 103 days per 100 students in a year, Hawaiian and Pacific Islander students 63 days, and Indigenous students 54 days compared to 21 days lost for white students.[5] In our own state of Massachusetts, Black girls are suspended 3.9 times more than white girls.[6] As with grading, we too often find ourselves blaming students for these disparities.

---

5 Daniel J. Losen and Paul Martinez, *Lost Opportunities: How Disparate School Discipline Continues to Drive Differences in the Opportunity to Learn* (Palo Alto, CA/Los Angeles, CA: Learning Policy Institute; Center for Civil Rights Remedies at the Civil Rights Project, UCLA, 2020).

6 *Appleseed Network: Protecting Girls of Color from the School-to-Prison Pipeline*, Appleseed Network, July 20, 2020, appleseednetwork.org/uploads/1/2/4/6/124678621/appleseed_network_-_protecting_girls_of_color_2020.pdf.

Efforts to dismantle discipline strategies need to be based on the foundational concept that school is a place where students should feel loved, supported, and safe. There are three aspects of our schools we can examine to see how they fail to create this safe environment for many students of color—building structure and environment, classroom culture, and school culture.

As leaders, we understand the complexity we face in our decision-making around discipline, and state and federal discipline policies have only made our roles more challenging. But fundamentally, as leaders, we set the tone for our school culture, and we need to take responsibility for shifting the tide of that culture toward love, inclusiveness, and safety.

Since the tragic school shooting at Columbine High School, school safety has focused on protecting those in the building from outsiders. Security companies have sold us on more security equipment, such as cameras and bulletproof glass, designed to keep outsiders out. Despite the increased security measures, school shootings have continued. Without a doubt, we need to make the best decisions for our schools to prevent these acts. However, if we are not mindful of the messages we are sending to students who already feel like outsiders, then the more armor and security we build up, the more students we push out. With an antiracist mindset, our policies should prioritize students' safety without excluding and further marginalizing students who already feel targeted as aggressors.

Utilizing an antiracist mindset when we consider school safety means ensuring we are thinking about safety for all. A safe school is a school in which all students feel safe. It is easy to overlook this aspect of safety when we are focused on making our buildings safer from outsiders. Research shows, for example, that the best way to address violence in schools is by creating an environment in which students can identify an adult they can go to.[7] This mindset not only helps us make

---

7 Sarah Lindstrom Johnson, "Improving the School Environment to Reduce School Violence: A Review of the Literature," *Journal of School Health* 79, no. 10 (2009): 451–465.

sure we are making decisions that allow students of color to feel safe in school, it also creates a priority that adults form positive connections with all students: a great example of how antiracist work is good for all students. When we are advocating for more resources, we should be considering social workers and school counselors.

There are a lot of opinions about the role school resource officers should play. Many decisions around this topic fall outside the decision-making power of the school or district administrators; however, it is clear that we as leaders need to invest in our relationships with police departments. We need to make sure they are focused on the same values we are as a school. It is also important to recognize that certain communities are rightfully more cautious and more suspicious of police departments due to national and local incidents of police violence against racialized communities. We have worked with school resource officers who have done a phenomenal job of buying into the school culture of love, welcome, and safety for all students. These youth officers have focused on three ideas:

1. Community building by knowing all students
2. Understanding themselves as educators
3. Agreeing to a memorandum of understanding that protects students—no arrests in school, no interrogating students without parents present

Establishing a relationship between the school district and the police is certainly outside the boundaries of the school leader's work. But as antiracist leaders who are creating a school culture, we need to push our supervisors and superintendents to develop a comprehensive relationship with the police that is student focused and prioritizes the values of antiracism. Additionally, consider joining the district safety team, which works with the police department in many districts.

Restorative practices

Restorative practices are the tools used to provide healing and repair when a harm has occurred. With research in law enforcement indicating that engaging restorative practices reduces recidivism rates, many schools have adopted at least some components of restorative practices.[8] Outside organizations have also emerged to support school districts as they incorporate restorative practices into the schools, namely providing opportunities for restorative circles.[9] Social justice education advocates have started to use restorative practices as a concept to address disparities and racism within our discipline structures.

If we are going to adopt this idea, then we need to incorporate restorative practices holistically, applying them in our daily work with students rather than as a tool to be used occasionally. This means incorporating restorative practices into every aspect of the culture and community. Restorative practices can be time-consuming and must be applied consistently in the classroom on a daily basis; that means using circles to start and close the week, creating shared values and agreements, and giving students a voice to resolve issues. What it does not mean is centering "order" and "authority." When a student violates an expectation, they learn that they have impacted the community. It may take years for visible results, but if done with integrity, you will see a decrease in discipline data and an increase in student efficacy.

If we are going to change the narrative on school discipline, we must invest in practices that are good for students, even if they take time.

Leveling/tracking

Levels remain a structure that encourages the persistence of racial disparities in our schools. Researchers have demonstrated that despite the fact that Black and Latinx students achieve when given the

---

8 Trevor Fronius et al., *Restorative Justice in US Schools: An Updated Research Review*, WestEd, March 2019, wested.org/resources/restorative-justice-in-u-s-schools-an-updated-research-review/.

9 As we seek to address societal ills such as racism, consider learning more about transformative justice versus restorative justice. A good book to start with is *Beyond Survival: Strategies and Stories from the Transformative Justice Movement*, eds. Leah Lakshmi Piepzna-Samarasinha and Ejeris Dixon, (Oakland, CA: AK Press, 2020).

opportunity to take advanced courses, these courses are not offered to them.[10] The benefit of heterogeneous grouping is that students learn together and interact with one another. We should be using culturally responsive instructional strategies in addition to strategies like differentiated instruction and universal design for learning to help scaffold our classes so that a diverse range of learners can learn together. When we create heterogeneous courses, students typically placed in lower-leveled classes need to feel and believe they are part of the class, not just welcome guests. In fact, they should be the focus, allowing stronger students the opportunity to learn and utilize skills to lift up their classmates. If we support students in developing antiracist skills, as described in chapter 8, then our heterogeneous groupings will incorporate effective adult and student skills to create a classroom where all are welcome and all will grow.

Leveling systems present their challenges in many ways. We have observed gifted and talented programs in elementary and middle schools with as many as 70 percent of students enrolled, and all of those students are white or Asian. Additionally, we have encountered rigid guidelines to enroll in a high school honors course that discourages students from even trying to take a more rigorous course.

Changing these structures is challenging for several reasons:

- A strong community belief in levels
- Skills gaps among students
- Lack of preparation for staff in teaching a heterogeneously grouped classroom

Making changes to levels requires a lot of fortitude, as resistance will be high. Therefore, make sure you have a clear message to explain why you are making changes. Identify the data you are using to assess this change. How many more students have access to honors or gifted

---

10 Kayla Patrick, Allison Rose Socol, and Ivy Morgan, "Inequities in Advanced Coursework," The Education Trust, January 9, 2020, edtrust.org/resource/inequities-in-advanced-coursework/; Sonali Kohli and Quartz, "Modern Day Segregation in Public Schools," *Atlantic*, November 18, 2014, theatlantic.com/education/archive/2014/11/modern-day-segregation-in-public -schools/382846/.

and talented learning through your change, or how are students demonstrating improvement through this change? Finally, take your time, as this kind of change requires so many other changes, as well, including incorporating diverse instructional strategies and having clear skill-learning outcomes in a course.

Changes to leveling reinforce the notion that equity work is messy work. But remember that antiracist schools do not seek to separate students. Rather they seek to focus on learning, love, and support. If you remember this, you will make it through the messy work.

Hiring practices

Hiring is the best way to shift and improve culture. But too often, we have seen hiring committees and principals focus on the wrong things, such as credentials and canned answers to predictable questions. Hiring committees often look for candidates who mirror the culture instead of enhancing the culture. Our hiring processes inform candidates about our culture. Many school districts use the strategy of having a screening or hiring committee ask the same questions to the candidates. We have been part of too many interviews where the focus is on the consistency of how questions are asked by the committee, and the interview becomes more about the questions than the candidate. Instead of showing off how our school is student centered and antiracist, we end up scaring away or even boring candidates of color by demonstrating how pretentious we are. As candidates, we have been put off by interview processes in which the committee is more interested in trying to trip us up with a convoluted question than how we answer the question. Why do we then do it to others when we are the interviewers?

Tips for Recruiting a Diverse Workforce

Recruitment:
- Be explicit and active in your recruitment goal to hire people of color.
- Research and utilize nontraditional platforms and events to seek candidates of color.

Inclusive Language:
- Create branding and marketing materials that highlight your school's commitment to antiracism and inclusion.
- In your job description, minimize language that prioritizes years of experience, credentials, and/or licensure and emphasize skills and experiences that speak to ability and adaptability to learn and grow in the job.
- Use gender-neutral and other inclusive language in your written and oral communication.

Interviewing:
- Interviews should reflect the diversity of your school/department, including the students it serves.
- Consider inviting support staff to join a hiring team to provide perspectives that may not exist among your teaching staff.

Retention:
- Support affinity groups for faculty and staff of color to assure a commitment to a safe and supportive working environment. Create opportunities for mentorship and professional growth to support a path of career advancement. Since this is long-term work, utilize feedback from your staff to continue improving every year.

It is no wonder, then, that despite principals who say they are committed to hiring diverse candidates, they make no progress. Hiring educators of color is challenging because we represent a small percentage of a candidate pool. In Massachusetts, only 14 percent of students in teacher preparation programs are people of color.[11] This is consistent with national data, which has found that around 80 percent of people in education preparation programs are white. This is particularly problematic when, by 2024, 54 percent of students will be people of color.[12] Nevertheless, when we do not demonstrate our values during the hiring process, we will not attract candidates of color. Therefore, antiracist principals need to create a hiring process that values antiracism and allows educators who share our values to shine.

Tips on Hiring People of Color

- Reduce bias in the screening process: Consider keeping candidate names anonymous to minimize unconscious bias in the hiring process.
- Consider a person's life experience as an asset. Many candidates of color share lived experiences with students of color. This should be viewed as a strength in their candidacy, not just an added bonus.
- Be mindful not to dismiss candidates based on antiquated and racist ideas of "professionalism," i.e., hairstyle, outfit, vernacular, etc. View the individual as a whole and consider how their cultural differences and perspectives could be beneficial to a homogeneous workforce and in improving representation for students.

---

11 "Diverse and Culturally Responsive Workforce," Massachusetts Department of Elementary and Secondary Education, updated June 16, 2021, doe.mass.edu/csi/diverse-workforce.

12 *The State of Racial Diversity in the Educator Workforce* (Washington, DC: US Department of Education, 2016), www2.ed.gov/rschstat/eval/highered/racial-diversity/state-racial-diversity-workforce.pdf.

- Ask questions that reflect the district's commitment to anti-racism and culturally responsive practices:
  - How have race and culture informed or impacted your work as an educator?
  - Please share a personal or professional experience that demonstrates how you've worked to understand perspectives of people whose cultural or racial background is different from your own.
  - How have your previous life, work, or educational experiences prepared you to educate students from diverse groups?
  - How do you honor your students' racial, ethnic, or cultural differences in your instructional pedagogy?
  - Sometimes there is a belief that a commitment to diversity conflicts with a commitment to excellence. How would you describe the relationship between diversity and excellence?[13]
  - Share your antiracist values and expectations with the candidates.

Until the pool for candidates of color increases, we will still have applicant pools that are largely white. In these situations, we should look for candidates who demonstrate the strengths of culturally responsive instruction and a passion for working in an antiracist environment. The more we hire people with these values, the more our culture will shift, which will then attract more candidates of color, as well.

---

13 "Sample Interview Questions: Diversity and Equity," Affirmative Action and Equity Compliance, Northern Illinois University, accessed March 2, 2022. niu.edu/diversity/_files/equal-opportunity/sample-interview-questions-diversity-and-equity.pdf

Conclusion

The policy areas and structures explored here are not an exhaustive list of areas where antiracist policies are needed. As we continue the cycle of inquiry, we are able to identify and understand where change is needed if we are to address the racism and inequity within the policy. But the policy issues described here demonstrate the many areas that need to be addressed. While addressing these policies, we need to keep in mind that changes need to be 1) driven by racial equity, 2) collaborative, and 3) continually assessed for effectiveness. If we do this, we will avoid the pitfalls of past equity changes and we will prioritize revising these policies, regardless of how hard it may be to do so.

KEY IDEAS

- Racist policies seek to separate students instead of focusing on the values of learning and love.
- Continue to use the cycle of inquiry as a model for change. Learn-reflect-act-assess. As our students change, our policies and structures need to change.
- Changing policies helps to change educator practices, as well, and therefore shift the culture.
- Policies such as grading, discipline, and leveling need to be aligned with student learning.
- Hiring practices need to demonstrate to candidates the culture we desire to create.

CHANGE THE NARRATIVE

LEARN–Read a book or watch a video on systemic inequities in schools. Some examples:

- Books: *Other People's Children* by Lisa Delpit, *So You Want to Talk about Race* by Ijeoma Oluo, *We Want to Do More Than Survive: Abolitionist Teaching and the Pursuit of Educational Freedom* by Bettina Love
- Videos: "Segregated by Design"[14]

REFLECT-What policy do you have to enforce that makes you the most uncomfortable?

ACT-Set a strategic plan for dismantling and changing a policy in your school.

ASSESS-Analyze data on a recent policy change or a current policy that you are looking to change. In what ways does that policy impact different students?

---

14 "Segregated by Design," directed by Mark Lopez (Austin, TX: Silkworm, 2019), segregatedbydesign.com/.

CHAPTER 11

ANTIRACIST COLLABORATION WITH FAMILIES AND THE COMMUNITY

There is no power for change greater than a community discovering what it cares about.

—MARGARET J. WHEATLEY

Despite best intentions, thoughtful training plans, or buy-in from the majority of staff, the work of antiracism in a school district does not come to full fruition without the collaboration of families and the community. Within a school community, children walk through the front doors with a foundation of culture and values that begins at home. Even when unconscious, bias shows up in the classroom, in the lunchroom, on teams and clubs, and in how students see themselves and others in the world. The school environment is an integral part of their learning development, but learning is best done in collaboration with and with the support of their parents and guardians. If students are learning something in the classroom, regardless of the topic, it is always helpful to have parents and guardians informed so they can supplement the content. Antiracism is no different. Expanding education and opportunities for parents and families to learn more about the work happening in their school district will help ground the values of inclusion, not only for students as they enter their school building, but also when they return home or are out and about in the community.

In many scenarios, parents may be your strongest allies, and in other cases, your loudest resisters.

In Kathy's role in her school district, family members frequently reach out to ask how they can be supportive and to share ideas and projects they are leading in partnership with their child's classroom teacher or within a racial justice family group they have organized. We will share some of these ideas throughout this chapter, but the conversations and meeting invitations are helpful for leaders as they offer educators the opportunity to better learn about the priorities of the parent community, and they also allow parents to get information about their child's experiences that may not have been shared elsewhere. On the other end of the spectrum are parents and community members who don't believe that schools should discuss race, and we receive those calls and emails, as well. These complaints center on the dominant culture of whiteness, not wanting comfort to be disrupted, and a belief that educating students to have a broader understanding of our history and of difference is harmful to "their" children. Learning to navigate both sides of this spectrum and including parents and partners as part of your comprehensive approach will move the work faster and further.

As we provide tips and strategies in this chapter, we encourage you to begin thinking about ways to include families and community members as part of a broader, comprehensive plan. Many of the components of this plan will mirror what we've shared in our work with students and staff but will be tailored to families. The strategic actions focused on families should include a plan for transparent communication, education programming, ways to empower families of color, and opportunities for co-conspirator family members to provide support in the schools. It is worth noting that families will have very different levels of involvement. While you may have some family members who are heavily involved and eager to do this work, there may be many well-intentioned people who are unable to engage due to other commitments or who are constrained by the realities of poverty (for example, working multiple jobs) and care responsibilities. We should be careful not to dismiss these parents as uninterested or apathetic. Figuring out how to make them aware of this work and engage them is the goal. Similarly, there may be a variety of reasons why families resist this work: some may be unaware that it is important, and others may be fixated on their own racist ideas. We must be steadfast in this work and help families understand why antiracist schools are good for all students.

Education is emotional work. As educators we come to this work with a focus on mission, and families come into this partnership with the same level of heightened emotions. With that comes the range of behaviors we experience when we work with parents. Utilizing a culturally responsive lens, our commitment to partner with parents cannot waiver. For example, when we create rigid leveling policies to slow down a parent who would seek to plow through an appeals process, there are other parents who will not advocate for their student because they are intimidated. Our role is to help families understand our core values as an antiracist school, which is a school that helps to empower families that are historically marginalized and partners with those who are traditionally empowered to address the inequities in our school. When most families are focused on their own child and their own lives, this can be very challenging and messy work. But it is through this focus on families and the larger community that we can break down the barriers of systemic racism beyond the walls of our school.

Communication

The importance of ongoing communication as a strategic component of your antiracist plan cannot be stressed enough. Throughout this book, we have included different strategies of communication that are essential for antiracist leadership, including listening and formal and informal communication. These are all essential to incorporate in your communication with families. By sharing consistent updates and acknowledgments, you reinforce the commitment to this work for your staff and students. With families, this communication will also provide a connection to the why, what, and how of the antiracist culture you are cultivating in their child's education and school environment.

As we continue to emphasize, this work is long term, and the more you engage families and community partners along the way, the stronger your coalition will be when faced with difficult situations regarding community pushback. This pushback can show up when a child comes home with an assignment or shares their class discussion about racism or current events. If your antiracist vision is shared in silos or not broadly communicated as a community priority that is inclusive of all members, it reduces opportunities to provide parents the context to support or understand how this connects to their students' schoolwork.

In developing and articulating your vision for this work, consider what families should know about how it is connected to your schools' values of inclusion and belonging for all students. Center your language around the desire for all students to feel safe and supported and on the point that this work benefits all students in learning about other cultures. Provide families with opportunities to learn more and ask questions, and ask for their support in supplementing this work at home through ongoing and age-appropriate conversations about race that will help students process big events that are impacting your district, state, or even country.

Often these messages are received with gratitude from parents and guardians who may have felt their children have been overlooked until now, but you can also expect responses that express dissatisfaction, and even anger, from parents or guardians who accuse you of politicizing an event or claim to fear that these discussions create more harm and trauma.

These opinions are generally centered on the historical safety and comfort of white people. Even though many white parents are apprehensive about talking to children about race, as discussed previously, we highlighted in a previous chapter how even infants identify race and make racial connections.[1] Avoiding these conversations prioritizes the dominant group's safety while minimizing (or dismissing) the need for the emotional safety of students of color or marginalized groups who are most significantly impacted.

Modes of communication with parents, guardians, and your broader community should vary to meet the needs and accessibility of your intended audience. To be as inclusive as possible, make a concerted effort to deliver your messages in a way that can be accessed by all in the community. There may be barriers for some families to receiving information, depending on their access to technology, work schedules, language needs, etc. Too often, this piece is overlooked and further excludes community members from equitable access to information. Take time to learn more about your parent community and ask them their preferred means of contact or the best ways to reach them.

Styles of communication with families should be varied and regular. For example, we have learned that some families receive information better through text message, while others prefer email. Additionally, interpreters are provided for families during meetings and back-to-school nights.

Family events can also provide opportunities to proactively connect with families. Fun community-building events, such as multicultural nights, can be a positive way to encourage families to connect with each other, to feel valued by their school, and to celebrate together. At our multicultural night, any family is welcome to prepare meals from their cultural backgrounds. Teachers, students, and families are welcome to attend and enjoy. While food makes everything better, the real power of the event is the intercultural exchange from families who typically do not interact with each other. Most importantly, though, leaders must connect such events to the school's antiracist work. We have found that these community events bring out families who do

---

1 Jess Sullivan, Leigh S. Wilton, and Evan Apfelbaum, "Adults Delay Conversations about Race Because They Underestimate Children's Processing of Race," preprint, July 18, 2020, doi. org/10.31234/osf.io/5xpsa.

not often attend other family events, and therefore we make sure to use these opportunities to inform families about the work we are doing and connect our message to antiracist practices. These regular forms of communication go a long way in helping all families understand the work being done in the school.

A focused communication strategy with families is perhaps the most important way to inform families. This is helpful for families when students engage with them about what they are learning. However, when it comes to talking about race and racism, it is also important to recognize that many families will feel underprepared to engage in these kinds of conversations. Some may respond with trepidation, while others may exhibit fear and anger. Furthermore, for our families who were born outside of the United States, their understanding of race may be very different depending on where they were born, and many of the US-created structures of systemic racism may feel strange and absurd—which they are. Therefore, having a clear education plan for families and the community should be an essential component to complement the work you are doing in your school.

Educating Families and the Community

Education is one of the few common experiences we all share. As adults, we are experts in our own educational experience and therefore have firm beliefs about what our child's education should look like (or should not look like). It can be striking how many parents or guardians have strong opinions about education when they have not set foot in a school in over twenty years, with the exception of back-to-school night. This is one of the reasons it can be so hard for some schools to change. Even though we discussed that schools have not changed structurally in more than a hundred years, some families believe that schools have changed in a variety of ways, such as our curriculum priorities, books we incorporate, and instructional strategies. It was particularly clear that many families were not aware of what was happening in our schools when the COVID-19 pandemic lockdown forced students to learn from home and they were challenged with helping their children learn.

When we focus on dismantling race and racism in schools, many families are going to feel challenged by this work, even if they agree with it. Therefore, having a comprehensive plan to educate families around antiracism is important to help them understand why we are focused on this work and to help them reinforce these ideas at home. Helping families learn how to have conversations about race with their children and understand the concepts we are teaching helps families buy into this work and feel more confident when they are talking about race and racism at home. We have heard many times that letting the school start the "sex talk" with your children helps to make that conversation less uncomfortable. We should view talking about race similarly, except that it will be more comfortable for some families to talk about than others.

Educating on Traditions

In many families, there are traditions and cultural values that stretch back through years, decades, and even centuries that become important markers for celebration, grieving, and transitions. Our understanding of these traditions can be limited because of a lack of exposure to or education about traditions outside those of the dominant culture. For example, in Cape Verdean culture, it is not uncommon for women to join in unison and wail for hours over the body of a loved one who has passed. This practice is common in other countries, as well, as a way to grieve in community and release emotions associated with sadness, pain, and/or anger, yet it is a practice rarely seen in our society. Without education about this ritual, it could be experienced as awkward, weird, or uncomfortable for those who are unfamiliar, which can subsequently propel feelings of shame and embarrassment for the one grieving. This is how we exclude members of our community and reinforce spaces that feel unwelcoming.

Embedding antiracist practices in your school includes dismantling many of the standards that center the dominant culture and expanding on practices and communication to be inclusive and representative of a diversity of traditions and cultural norms. This is done by learning more about the students and families that make up your school community and inviting all to share the values that are important to them. This can be done by sending out a survey to your parent community about holidays, traditions, and religious practices. The information gathered can help you produce broader communication that will support educators in teaching students about diverse cultures and honoring practices that may impact student performance, such as fasting during Ramadan (a thirty-day ritual honored by Muslims) or long school absences during shiva (a seven-day mourning period in Judaism).

Food is often connected to celebration and can be a wonderful way to engage community members through sharing recipes and traditions of cooking, such as the common practice in Puerto Rican and other Latin American cultures of making pasteles during the Christmas season. This labor-intensive process can take several days and usually involves many hands of family members and friends. Exploring and celebrating traditions will not only create a more welcoming space for students and families of all backgrounds, it will also introduce new ideas and traditions to other students and families that will hopefully expand their knowledge and curiosity about difference. This then helps us become more aware of narratives and practices that only center one culture as dominant and standard and continue to marginalize those who have other stories and experiences.

Educating on Curriculum

Providing information about your vision of antiracism and the benefits of children learning how to discuss race and racism at an early age will help keep parents informed and hopefully invested in their child's growth in this area. We know from research that children as young as three months are able to show a preference for own-race faces over other-race faces.[2] Knowing this, we have a responsibility as educators to do our best to make sure all children feel safe, seen, understood, valued, and capable. Not only must we challenge ourselves to open up spaces for children to have honest conversations about race, we must remind parents and guardians that we are all responsible for supporting a safe community for all children. This means holding those conversations at home, as well.

Much of this language and these concepts are still new and evolving, which can create confusion and mistrust from families and community members. Concepts and definitions such as antiracism and equity might appear to be self-explanatory on the surface, but that does not mean there is a universal understanding of what it looks like in practice. Hosting parent nights and community events is a great way to educate and inform families and the broader community of what this work will look like in classrooms and in the overall school culture. Using this language in your regular communication supports families as they come to understand these terms, as well.

We have used our Parent Teacher Student Organization (PTSO) to host our education programs for families to help send the message that this work is community focused. In turn, we have seen a steady increase in families engaging in this work. However, it is worth noting that focusing on education may tend to attract many families who feel the least informed on matters around race and racism. This is a crucial group of families to connect with, however, it may not attract

---

2 David J. Kelly et al. "Three-Month-Olds, but Not Newborns, Prefer Own-Race Faces," *Developmental Science* 8, no. 6 (2005): F31–F36.

communities of color because the information is so basic. Therefore, in addition to a comprehensive education plan, making sure you have a clear plan for engaging with communities of color is essential, as well.

Families are vital partners who want success for their children and can be invaluable assets to student learning. With strong communication and trust in place, all families can provide unique insight to teachers, help students set and work toward goals, and support ongoing learning and exploration at home.

This communication will help families and community partners understand why this work is critical for ALL students and highlight the steps your school is taking to become antiracist. It will encourage participants to examine individual and group biases, discuss antiracist values and practices, and come up with ways for parents and community members to partner in this work as allies.

LEARN: How families and community stakeholders can partner with schools to address issues that might be affecting schools and community members and to elevate the message and practice of antiracism at home.

REFLECT: What questions do you have about the changes happening in your child's school? What steps did you take to confirm the information you had was accurate? Did you approach the issue in support of the change or as an adversary? Was your approach productive?

ACT: Organize a time for families to meet with school leaders to learn more about the mission and purpose of your school's antiracist practices. Ask how you can be supportive and create opportunities to engage and inform other community members and stakeholders via information forums, webinars, creating learning communities, book clubs, raising funds, etc.

Empowering Families of Color

Transformational leaders understand the need to encourage and motivate families in order to engage them in the changes they envision. For families of color, you can provide opportunities for their voices to be invited and included as part of planning and goal setting. Soliciting their feedback and creating spaces for them to share their experiences, their challenges, and their hopes will not only develop partners in the work, but will help you prioritize areas of the work that will have the most impact. For many families of color, this may be the first time their input has been sought, and they will be excited to participate; others may be skeptical. This is where the ongoing work of building relationships and remaining consistent is crucial.

When COVID-19 first emerged, the country went into lockdown and schools were operating remotely. Eventually, schools began to open their doors to students and families who were ready to transition back to in-person learning. In our experience, many families made the choice to return to school, but a significant number of families of color opted to have their children remain remote for a variety of personal reasons.

During this time, members of the parent community began to raise concerns that the difference between in-person and remote learning was inequitable and negatively impacted families of color in a disproportionate manner. In an attempt to learn more, a survey was designed to gather family input so that specific issues would be highlighted and addressed. The initial results of the survey showed limited engagement from families of color and provided little information about their experiences. The team needed to regroup and consider why families of color were not inclined to engage in an electronic survey meant to solicit their voices. After more planning and discussion, time limitations, mistrust, and accessibility were raised as potential barriers for certain families. A collaborative decision was made to reach out to each family individually and have a more personal dialogue about their child's experience as a remote learner, as well as their experience as a parent.

Several important connections were made through this process. The first was that there was overwhelming engagement from families when they were called and asked to share stories, rather than select boxes on an impersonal form. Families frequently commented on how much they appreciated a phone call and the opportunity to have a conversation that felt richer and more valuable. The second was that the majority of parents of color who were called expressed how much their child enjoyed the remote option, and some students were thriving in comparison to previous years of in-person learning. Yes, there were some areas that needed attention and there were some parents who did raise concerns, but not to the extent of the initial parent group who brought this to the broader district-level attention.

This process highlighted the need to engage all families and to consider multiple ways of gathering feedback, hearing voices, and empowering those who are often marginalized. Below are additional ways to consider learning more to address racist and inequitable practices and circumstances.

Surveys

Surveys are a quick and easy way to reach a large number of parents and guardians. Although you will never get a perfect response rate, you will be able to take the pulse on whether you are going in the right direction or if you need to pause and do more work in communicating your ideas and values. You may have to send the survey out several times or enlist your leaders who have developed stronger relationships with these families to do more targeted outreach.

A step further would be to identify staff that can reach out directly to parents and guardians of color via phone or in person to ask the survey questions more directly. With families where English is not the primary language, we use a text messaging app that allows us to alert families of the survey in their home language. Although this method requires more time, it can be more engaging for families to have a personal connection while sharing their experiences. It may also elicit more detail and context for you to better understand what would be helpful for these families.

Focus Groups

Focus groups are another way to gather more qualitative data and create spaces of camaraderie and community to learn more about authentic experiences. Unlike surveys, which gather limited individual input, focus groups allow you to ask follow-up questions, read the emotions and passion in the room, and also create an informal affinity space for families.

Your focus groups should be structured with at least one facilitator and have simple, direct questions that will provide you with helpful information. The facilitator's responsibility is to explain the purpose of the focus group and your plans for the information you will gather, create norms that allow people to feel safe sharing honest feedback without fear of repercussion, and to redirect the group back to its purpose if the conversation begins to veer off in a direction that isn't constructive. Having a skilled facilitator is ideal, but for those to whom this is new, consider using a resource like "The Art of Facilitating Focus Groups" to help you prepare.[3]

Regardless of your feedback methods, it is imperative that you communicate your values and the intent of your invitation, as well as your plans for the feedback. It is also essential that you follow through. This will help build trust and demonstrate that the group was not just a performative gesture.

In addition to getting feedback, inviting and empowering families of color to lead discussions, host events, or sit on panels are all ways to

---

3 *The Art of Facilitating Focus Groups*, National Consortium of Interpreter Education Centers, July 2011, interpretereducation.org/wp-content/uploads/2015/02/NCIEC_focus_group_manual_07-20112.pdf.

indicate that you want this work to be inclusive of their voices and that you recognize the value of their perspectives on education in the larger school community. This can also be demonstrated by including families of color in the interviewing and decision-making process for new hires, adding or changing after-school programs, revising class schedules, updating policies and more. Families can bring new perspectives to many aspects of their child's experiences that school administration can benefit from hearing, and they can be valuable partners, particularly in matters that will impact their child's school experience.

Creating a Parent Organization

For any school leader, support from the community will make this work more sustainable and impactful. One productive and effective way to engage parents and guardians is to invest some time and energy in helping them form a parent organization that is in line with your antiracist vision statement. In some school districts, these organizations may already exist, as we have seen an increase in community members forming racial or social justice groups over the last few years. A quick assessment of what already exists in your community will help you determine whether you can partner with an existing organization or bring others together to help support the initiation of a new one.

Along with other school leaders, set up a time to meet with parents and guardians who have expressed an interest in supporting an antiracist school plan. It is important that any organization interested in partnership is clear on your vision and sees themselves as amplifiers of your message committed to doing corresponding work in their parent community. Also, listen to parents to identify where mutual priorities exist and where partnership could be most beneficial, then create a plan together. Having a clear understanding and mutual agenda and making sure parents are kept apprised of the accomplishments and challenges you are experiencing will help minimize miscommunication and opportunities for adversarial positions.

As a director of diversity, equity, and inclusion, Kathy has monthly meetings with the leaders of the district's parent organization to check in and highlight priority areas that need to be addressed. In these meetings, members often express concerns over information they have gathered from other parents in various schools. Examples may include a need for a better response when racist incidents occur, or for better communication to the broader community about the incident and about what parents can do at home. Other agenda items may center on a need for more education for parents to be able to support the district's work or even an invitation to speak to a larger parent community about changes and updates related to antiracist practices.

With many of our parent organizations, we have experienced positive and effective collaboration when there is support for school leaders. They can be crucial in galvanizing broader support for school policy and protocol changes by using monthly meetings to discuss the benefits of the proposed change. Other activities can include districtwide forums to share updates on the work that has been accomplished and the work that continues to be prioritized or facilitating parent workshops that align with the training you are providing to your educators and staff.

As a principal, Henry also has a strong relationship with his parent organization that helps foster support for the implementation of policy and procedure changes by hosting forums for other parents and showing up to important community meetings to show solidarity. For an individual school, this group has also been helpful in organizing family events, such as Culture Night, Black Lives Matter Week, and other family engagement activities that support a welcoming and inclusive environment. Additionally, as concerns were raised in the media about affinity groups, this parent group organized a night for families to hear from staff and students of color about the importance of these groups in school.

Consider resources that will be needed to sustain a partnership. This may include a meeting space, contact list of other parents who may be interested, access to calendars so planning can coincide with school initiatives and events, and support messaging about their organization and values to the broader school community via your school communication methods. Check-in meetings with the organization should be consistent to ensure they are abreast of the current climate in your school, including racist incidents or changes to policies and procedures. In these meetings, a plan to harness the organization's support is critical to the comprehensive plan we discussed at the beginning of the chapter. It should also serve as time to invite feedback about your work as a leader and to highlight areas of need that remain. Like any partnership, there may be push and pull about priorities and resolutions, but open and honest conversations will help move the work along with transparency and consideration of potential blind spots.

Conclusion

The internal work you are doing within your school will only strengthen with support from the broader community. Change can be difficult and for it to be effective and transparent, your antiracist leadership practices must include consistency, communication, and education for families and stakeholders.

Families in your school community can be tremendous partners in this work if you are investing your time and energy in keeping them informed and providing opportunities for them to learn and understand the direction you are taking. Encourage families to learn alongside their children and empower them to have a voice and to be leaders in their own communities.

KEY IDEAS

- Collaboration with parents, guardians, and community partners is an important component to your success.

- Clear and ongoing communication about your school's antiracist values and vision will provide context for your work.
- Parent organizations can be effective partners in amplifying your vision and holding their communities accountable.

CHANGE THE NARRATIVE

LEARN-About the different stakeholders and organizations in your school community that share an antiracist commitment and can become partners.

REFLECT-What are the biggest criticisms you face from your parent community, and how can you engage them in learning more?

ACT-Determine a consistent and frequent mode of communication with your parent and partner communities to keep them informed of your vision and the work that is happening. Create opportunities for the community to complement the learning you are providing your educators and students

ASSESS-Engage families of color to actively provide feedback and share their experiences through surveys, focus groups, and individual conversation.

CONCLUSION

Throughout this book we have discussed the learning, reflection, actions, and assessments that build and reinforce an antiracist culture. We have also included specific initiatives, strategies, and policy changes that we propose implementing to dismantle old practices and structures and replace them with antiracist ones. We have shared personal stories about the challenges and successes we have experienced, as well as the support and resistance that present themselves whenever a leader attempts to shift the longstanding culture in any school or organization. So how do we know that the culture is changing in the right direction? How do we know if we are actually changing the narrative?

Over time, we have witnessed more and more students, staff, families, and community members join us on the journey—many of whom have ended up taking on leadership roles in this work. An antiracist culture has many antiracist leaders, and it was inspiring when our school community started to gain confidence in reflecting on their own relationship with race and racism and to advocate for racial justice. We see this as a step in the right direction.

Certainly, there are data points we pay attention to, e.g., racial diversity in courses, clubs, and activities; grade data of marginalized groups; connectedness data; hate crime and incident data; and racial makeup of faculty, to name a few. There is progress to be excited about, as well as areas where growth remains slow. We must pay attention to both. What we hold as a clear sign that our culture is shifting in the right direction is the commitment to progress in these areas and recognition of our individual responsibility—and it is important that these developments are acknowledged and celebrated.

For us, these are a few moments where we are seeing the narrative change:

- English and theater programs have both designed performances that highlight the voices of students of color.
- Every member of our sixteen-person administrative team identified a specific initiative in their unique role to implement culturally responsive instruction and address racism in our school.
- Black, Latinx, Asian, and South Asian student affinity groups worked together to host a united assembly.
- Our parent group—Families Organizing for Racial Justice (FORJ)—planned a citywide event for Juneteenth.
- A self-directed faculty committee emerged to address more antiracist and equitable grading practices.
- A group of predominantly white teachers created a subgroup to reflect on their own involvement with racism and ways to help our school.
- Every department took on work to improve their curriculum and instruction around antiracist skills and to increase the number of multilevel courses.
- A white-student-led environmental group made a commitment to racial justice in environmental policy.

There are so many other moments we could note here, but what stands out is the demonstration of sustained work and the arrival of new leaders to this work. Our antiracist culture is becoming embedded in and central to our school culture.

Where Do We Go from Here?

A few years back, Henry listened to a retired superintendent who was involved with antiracism in education in the 1980s and 1990s as he shared some of the work the district was doing at that time. During that presentation and after, Henry grew frustrated as he reflected on how the district and his school today were working on the same issues the district was working on thirty years earlier—leveling, hiring diverse faculty, grading. Literally it was as if the ideas were lifted from the current school improvement plan or district strategic plan. Had they not made any progress?

When Henry shared his frustration with another school leader who had worked in the district during that earlier time, she replied that they were still working on the same goals because people retreated from the work as conversations about race became too intense. School and district leaders focused on other topics, and teachers focused on their individual practice. The commitment to teaching all students remained, but steadily the district lost focus on the fight that is required of an antiracist district.

This speaks to how emotional and frustrating antiracist work can be and how antiracist culture is not permanent if we do not continue to lean into this work. We have to work for the culture we want, even when the path of least resistance is to avoid acknowledging racism and prioritize other issues in our schools—when it feels more productive to take on problems that seem to have easy and clear solutions.

The reality is that the less we try to fight racism, the more entrenched and incessant it becomes. Schools are currently facing strong resistance from organized movements of parents, politicians, and activists who are trying to scare educators away from talking about racism with students. States are passing laws banning books and any teaching about racism; people are running for school committees claiming that schools are making white students feel bad about them-selves; and white families are getting messages that critical race theory is indoctrinating their children.[1] It is clear that this is an attempt to keep educators from engaging in the work to dismantle systemic racism in their schools. And what we have seen too often with movements such as these is their success in silencing voices and creating racist policies.

This does not mean that we should back away from our work to foster an antiracist school culture—it means that our commitment must be unwavering in the face of adversity. Kathy and a group of Massachusetts DEI leaders wrote in an op-ed in the *Boston Globe*, "Speaking about the impacts of race and racism is not inherently racist, and not talking about racism doesn't make it disappear."[2] It is quite possible that this organized attack on schools will result in students of color feeling more disconnected, and in some schools there will be an increase in hate incidents. Rather than succumb to the pressures of this movement, we must dig in our heels and continue to educate the community, counteract misinformation and expand our allyship.

To move past racism is to talk about racism and usually the tensest moments are the same moments when progress occurs. Antiracist leadership means having a growth mindset about students, ourselves, and our colleagues. Antiracist leadership means recognizing our individual responsibility and the collective responsibility to fight racism. Antiracist leadership means taking action to make change in our practice and to make change in our structures and systems.

Committing to making a school an antiracist school is no small task. At the same time, making wholesale change to our individual practice and our school all at once is never successful. What we are certain of is that *the status quo is not acceptable.* We must take an approach that is sustained, allows for missteps and learning, and is inclusive and

---

1   Tat Bellamy-Walker, "Book Bans in Schools Are Catching Fire. Black Authors Say Uproar Isn't about Students," NBC online, January 6, 2022, nbcnews.com/news/nbcblk/book-ban s-schools-are-catching-fire-black-authors-say-uproar-isnt-stud-rcna10228; Rashawn Ray and Alexandra Gibbons, "Why Are States Banning Critical Race Theory?," *FixGov*, The Brookings Institution, November 2021, brookings.edu/blog/fixgov/2021/07/02/why-are-states-bannin g-critical-race-theory/.

2   Massachusetts DEI directors, "Diversity, Equity, and Inclusion Should Be Included in Schools," *Boston Globe*, updated July 5, 2021, bostonglobe.com/2021/07/05/opinion/diversity-equity -inclusion-education-should-be-included-public-schools/.

adaptable to the messiness of this work. Throughout this work, we need to maintain our focus on a growth mindset and stay optimistic about our progress.

Bending toward Justice

We subscribe to the philosophy that Martin Luther King Jr. described and that was later popularized by President Obama: "The arc of the moral universe is long, but it bends toward justice."[3] This philosophy has been criticized by writers like Ta-Nehisi Coates, because it seems too optimistic to believe that we will stand up to racist resistance. Coates said to *Vox* in 2016, "But when you study civilizations, it tends to be true that history has a weight, a gravity—if you're going to go in an opposite direction, you need to consciously exercise an opposite force. And I don't see us doing that."[4] While we agree with Coates that the moral arc of the universe is not inevitable, we believe that there are enough of us committed to this work to make it successful. It is our experience that even when resistance to racial progress occurs in schools, there are those of us who sustain the work in spite of it. We are the troublemakers—the good troublemakers.

Looking back to the story of the superintendent from the 1980s and 1990s, we see the purpose of the pushback a bit differently than when Henry first heard the story. We know that during the time of this pushback, there were educators throughout the district who continued this work on their own. There were teachers who centered antiracism in their classrooms and school leaders who strategically worked on dismantling racist policies. While the entire district may not have focused on this work, there were people throughout who were keeping the work alive. They were creating good trouble. It is this good trouble that keeps antiracist work going even when we face mounting resistance.

---

3 Martin Luther King Jr., "Remaining Awake through a Great Revolution," speech delivered at the National Cathedral, Washington, DC, March 31, 1968.

4 Ta-Nehisi Coates, interview by Ezra Klein from *The Ezra Klein Show, Vox*, December 19, 2016, vox.com/conversations/2016/12/19/13952578/ta-nehisi-coates-ezra-klein.

John Lewis was only twenty-one when he led the Student Nonviolent Coordinating Committee in 1961. He was just a few years older than our students when he began his activism and helped to lead the freedom rides. In a commencement address he gave at Emory University in 2014, he said:

> The action of Rosa Parks and the words and leadership of Dr. King inspired me to find a way to get in the way. I got in the way. I got in trouble. Good trouble, necessary trouble.
>
> You must leave here and go out and get in the way. When you see something that is not right, not fair, not just, you must have the courage to stand up, to speak up, and find a way to get in the way.
>
> When I was your age, some maybe thought I was just a little off. Maybe a little maladjusted. But sometimes you have to be a little maladjusted. Stood in the way of peace, stood in the way of love, stood in the way of nonviolence, and students, during the late 50s and early 60s, we came together. . . . By sitting in, by sitting down, we were standing up for the very best in American tradition.

When faced with all of this hate, resistance, and injustice, he said:

> We didn't give up. We didn't give in. We didn't lose faith. We kept our eyes on the prize. And as students, as graduates, you must keep your eyes on the prize. You have a moral obligation, a mission, and a mandate to do your part. You must play a role, help to redeem the soul of America, help create a beloved America, a beloved world where no one is left out or left behind

because of their race or their class. In the final analysis, we are one people. We are one family.[5]

We should expect resistance to manifest when we fight racism—historically, it always has. Yet, it is just as important to remember that it is a
necessary part of the work, and with resistance, we are forced to pause
and reflect on our strategy and impact—it allows us to become clearer
in our purpose and more determined to push through.

Can we trust our colleagues, students, and families to continue
with this work when the resistance becomes more intense and more
personal? We believe many will. There are many educators, students,
and families who understand that complex structural change is hard,
time-consuming, and endless. But they also understand that the status
quo is not acceptable, and they are ready to confront the work. We just
have to help each other do it, together.

The work of an antiracist educator is to keep coming back to this
work and to continue to recommit. However, the work of an antiracist
leader is also to inspire and help others do the same. To be antiracist
leaders, we must be open to changing both our individual practice
and the structures of our school. The change must be daily work that
includes both reflection and risk-taking, and it will most definitely
involve making mistakes. We must do all of this work in the face
of resistance.

We believe that we are in a special moment in education. Moving
past the COVID-19 pandemic gives us an opportunity to reimagine
our schools and see the possibility. We are asking you to be color
brave rather than colorblind and to remain committed to making our
schools welcoming to all students—especially those who feel the most
marginalized. We have new opportunities to shift our practices and
school structures to make them more antiracist than our status quo.
A fear of change can paralyze us the same way our fear of being racist
can. A fear of the resistance can keep us from taking risks.

---

5 "Remembering John Lewis," Emory News Center, Emory University, July 23, 2020, news.emory.
edu/features/2020/07/remembering-john-lewis/index.html.

It is good for our school cultures if we disagree on solutions to these structural inequities, and it is just as important that we listen to the diversity of opinions. What we cannot disagree on is our purpose—that structural racism does, in fact, exist in our educational systems and that all students have a right to feel safe and welcomed in their learning environment. The more we are fighting racism, the more we will notice the bend in the arc of the universe. And although justice may still feel far away, progress can always be found if you are looking.

Maintain that optimism, work collaboratively, and create change. We got this. We're in this work together!

RESOURCES

Articles

"Adults Delay Conversations about Race Because They Underestimate Children's Processing of Race," by Jess Sullivan, Leigh Wilton, and Evan P. Apfelbaum, *Journal of Experimental Psychology*, August 6, 2020

"The Bias Detective," by Douglas Starr, *Science*, March 27, 2020

"Categorical Inequalities between Black and White Students Are Common in US Schools—But They Don't Have to Be," by Kenneth Shores, Ha Eun Kim, and Mela Still, *Brown Center Chalkboard*, The Brookings Institution, February 21, 2020

"Cultural Humility: Essential Foundation for Clinical Researchers," by Katherine A. Yeager and Susan Bauer-Wu, *Applied Nursing Research*, August 6, 2013

"Inequality at School," by Kirsten Weir, *Monitor on Psychology*, November 2016

"Inequities in Advanced Coursework," by Kayla Patrick, Allison Rose Socol, and Ivy Morgan, The Education Trust, January 9, 2020

"Mental Health among Asian-Americans," Koko Nishi, *Students' Corner*, American Psychological Association, 2012

"The Racial School Climate Gap: Within-School Disparities in Students' Experiences of Safety, Support, and Connectedness," by Adam Voight, Thomas Hanson, Meagan O'Malley, and Latifah Adekanye, *American Journal of Community Psychology*, December 2015

"Raising Race-Conscious Children: How to Talk to Kids about Race
and Racism," by Beata Mostafavi, *Children's Health*, Michigan
Medicine, July 22, 2020

"The Role of White Co-Conspirators in Dismantling Systemic
Racism," by Andrew Greenia, *Embracing Equity*, November
2, 2018

"What Is White Privilege, Really?," by Cory Collins, Learning for
Justice, Fall 2018

"Where Did They Go?: Retention Rates for Students of Color at
Predominantly White Institutions," by Kevin S. McClain and
April Perry, *College Student Affairs Leadership*, Spring 2017

"Why You Should Make Time for Self-Reflection (Even If You Hate
Doing It)," by Jennifer Porter, *Harvard Business Review*, March
21, 2017

Books

Anti-Bias Education for Young Children and Ourselves, by Louise
Derman-Sparks and Julie Olsen Edwards

Appreciative Inquiry: A Positive Revolution in Change, by David L.
Cooperrider and Diana Whitney

*Biased: Uncovering the Hidden Prejudice that Shapes What We See,
Think, and Do*, by Jennifer L. Eberhardt

*Culturally Responsive Teaching and the Brain: Promoting Authentic
Engagement and Rigor among Culturally and Linguistically Diverse
Students*, by Zaretta Hammond

Dare to Lead: Brave Work. Tough Conversations. Whole Hearts., by
Brené Brown

Difficult Conversations: How to Discuss What Matters Most, by
Douglas Stone, Bruce Patton, and Sheila Heen

*Evolving Learner: Shifting from Professional Development to
Professional Learning from Kids, Peers, and the World*, by Lainie
Rowell, Kristy Andre, and Lauren Steinmann

How to Be an Antiracist, by Ibram X. Kendi
So You Want to Talk About Race, by Ijeoma Oluo
Sustainable Leadership, by Andy Hargreaves and Dean Fink
Tinkering toward Utopia: A Century of Public School Reform, by David
    B. Tyack and Larry Cuban
Whistling Vivaldi: How Stereotypes Affect Us and What We Can Do,
    Claude M. Steele
*Why Are All the Black Kids Sitting Together in the Cafeteria?: And
Other Conversations about Race*, by Beverly Daniel Tatum

Reports

Restorative Justice in US Schools, WestEd, by Trevor Fronius, Sean
    Darling-Hammond, Hannah Persson, Sarah Guckenburg, Nancy
    Hurley, and Anthony Petrosino
Stop AAPI Hate National Report: 3/19/20–6/19/21, by Aggie J. Yellow
    Horse, Russell Jeung, Richard Lim, Boaz Tang, Megan Im, Lauryn
    Higashiyama, Layla Schweng, Mikayla Chen

Websites

edweek.org
facinghistory.org
learningforjustice.org
stopaapihate.org

ACKNOWLEDGMENTS

From Henry

Sarah and Grace: Thank you for the support and encouragement throughout this process. Sarah, thank you for your partnership and trust; I love you. Grace, I can't wait to see what the future holds for you.

Mom and Dad, the Turner, Ryan, Newell, Buchs, Palen, and Beard families: Thank you for the encouragement throughout this experience. Your regular questions about how this book was coming always helped me work through ideas and clarify our challenges.

Newton North Staff: Your passion for ALL kids inspires me every day. The stories in this book are our stories. The principal of Newton North is my dream job, and I hope that I give you at least a fraction of what you give me.

Finally, thank you to Kathy for your partnership on this journey. During the challenging moments and moments of joy, our North Star of this book was always clear. I have learned so much from you.

From Kathy

This book arrived as a gift. Henry, thank you for trusting me and for your invitation to join forces. Your drive, passion, and commitment to this work and your students are like no other. I learned so much through our partnership of sharing stories, challenging each other for the sake of a better product, and all of the laughs and small wins along the way. We did it!

To my family and friends, who never cease to show up when it matters—regardless of the endeavor. Thank you for the unequivocal support, especially in the moments where I doubted myself or was carrying the weight of deadlines. I wrote so many pieces of this book hoping you would feel seen.

To my father, Djodjoi, whose lifelong love of learning has never been lost on me. Thank you for dreaming so big for us that there was no choice but to rise to your expectations.

From Us

It is an honor to work in Newton. Thank you to the students, staff, and families for making this system an incredible place to learn and work. Our commitment to racial equity is unwavering and a model for others.

To our DBC team: Dave, Shelley, Tara, Lindsey, and all, thank you for your unwavering support from beginning to end. Throughout this process, you saw the need for this book, and without a doubt it is a better book because of you.

Thank you to all of you who provided suggestions, edits, and feedback along the way: Lorena German, Roberto German, David Fleishman, Toby Romer, Jennifer Letourneau, Ayesha Farag, Jessica Payne, Ine Ogagan, Diana Guzzi, Amy Winston, Charmie Curry, Joseph Corazzini, Traci Browder, Zachary Wright, Hedreich Nichols, Johnny Cole, Dwight Carter, Tom Murray, Beth Houf, Katie Martin, Nili Bartley, Linda Lopes, Ericka Jones, Andrea Beane, Bethany Lyons, Kerry Gallagher, Lainie Rowell, Michelle Leong, and Brianna Hodges.

ABOUT HENRY J. TURNER AND KATHY LOPES

Henry J. Turner, EdD

Henry J. Turner serves as principal at Newton North High School in Newton, Massachusetts. He is most proud of the collaborative community he works within to empower students to fight hate and bigotry in *their* school. Pointing to his unwavering commitment to equity and a student-centered culture, Henry was named 2020 K–12 Principal of the Year by the industry news site *K–12 Dive*.

A national speaker, Henry shares his experience as an innovative instructional leader, passionate advocate, and committed antiracist. Henry works with educators, leaders, and communities on how to create a culture that commits to diversity, equity, and inclusion, empowers students' voices, and addresses economic and racial disparities.

Henry is an instructor at the Educator Leadership Institute (ELI). He serves on the University of Massachusetts Commonwealth Honors College Advisory Board and the Massachusetts School Administrators' Association Board. He received his doctorate in education from Boston College, a master's in education from Framingham State University, and an undergraduate degree in history from the University of Massachusetts Amherst. He has a biweekly newsletter, *Lessons on Social Justice Leadership*.

Kathy Lopes, LICSW

Kathy Lopes is a clinical social worker and educator with over twenty years of experience ranging throughout primary, secondary, and post-secondary education. She currently serves as the director of diversity, equity, and inclusion for Newton Public Schools in Newton, Massachusetts, leading the district's work in their anti-racist leadership practices and principles. Additionally, she holds a long-standing adjunct faculty position at her alma mater, Simmons University School of Social Work.

Lopes is known as a local and national public speaker on topics of cultural humility, racial identity, and antiracism in education and mental health organizations. Recognized early in her career by the US Department of Justice with the Justice for Victims of Crime Award, social justice and equity have remained a consistent part of her leadership and strategic planning vision.

Additional Resources

For a study guide and additional resources please go to
henryjturner.com/changethenarrative.

Henry and Kathy offer joint and separate workshops, book study,
and speaking opportunities. To inquire:

Henry J. Turner
henry@henryjturner.com

Kathy Lopes
inKLusionconsulting.com

To take a companion online course,
please check out this link or QR code:
henryjturner.com/course

MORE FROM

DAVE BURGESS Consulting, Inc.

Since 2012, DBCI has published books that inspire and equip educators to be their best. For more information on our titles or to purchase bulk orders for your school, district, or book study, visit **DaveBurgessConsulting.com/DBCIbooks**.

Like a PIRATE™ Series

Teach Like a PIRATE by Dave Burgess
eXPlore Like a PIRATE by Michael Matera
Learn Like a PIRATE by Paul Solarz
Plan Like a PIRATE by Dawn M. Harris
Play Like a PIRATE by Quinn Rollins
Run Like a PIRATE by Adam Welcome
Tech Like a PIRATE by Matt Miller

Lead Like a PIRATE™ Series

Lead Like a PIRATE by Shelley Burgess and Beth Houf
Balance Like a PIRATE by Jessica Cabeen, Jessica Johnson, and
    Sarah Johnson
Lead beyond Your Title by Nili Bartley
Lead with Appreciation by Amber Teamann and Melinda Miller
Lead with Culture by Jay Billy
Lead with Instructional Rounds by Vicki Wilson
Lead with Literacy by Mandy Ellis
She Leads by Dr. Rachael George and Majalise W. Tolan

Leadership & School Culture

Beyond the Surface of Restorative Practices by Marisol Rerucha

Choosing to See by Pamela Seda and Kyndall Brown

Culturize by Jimmy Casas

Discipline Win by Andy Jacks

Escaping the School Leader's Dunk Tank by Rebecca Coda and Rick Jetter

Fight Song by Kim Bearden

From Teacher to Leader by Starr Sackstein

If the Dance Floor Is Empty, Change the Song by Joe Clark

The Innovator's Mindset by George Couros

It's OK to Say "They" by Christy Whittlesey

Kids Deserve It! by Todd Nesloney and Adam Welcome

Let Them Speak by Rebecca Coda and Rick Jetter

The Limitless School by Abe Hege and Adam Dovico

Live Your Excellence by Jimmy Casas

Next-Level Teaching by Jonathan Alsheimer

The Pepper Effect by Sean Gaillard

Principaled by Kate Barker, Kourtney Ferrua, and Rachael George

The Principled Principal by Jeffrey Zoul and Anthony McConnell

Relentless by Hamish Brewer

The Secret Solution by Todd Whitaker, Sam Miller, and Ryan Donlan

Start. Right. Now. by Todd Whitaker, Jeffrey Zoul, and Jimmy Casas

Stop. Right. Now. by Jimmy Casas and Jeffrey Zoul

Teachers Deserve It by Rae Hughart and Adam Welcome

Teach Your Class Off by CJ Reynolds

They Call Me "Mr. De" by Frank DeAngelis

Thrive through the Five by Jill M. Siler

Unmapped Potential by Julie Hasson and Missy Lennard

When Kids Lead by Todd Nesloney and Adam Dovico

Word Shift by Joy Kirr

Your School Rocks by Ryan McLane and Eric Lowe

Technology & Tools

50 Things to Go Further with Google Classroom by Alice Keeler and Libbi Miller

50 Things You Can Do with Google Classroom by Alice Keeler and
    Libbi Miller

140 Twitter Tips for Educators by Brad Currie, Billy Krakower, and
    Scott Rocco

Block Breaker by Brian Aspinall

Building Blocks for Tiny Techies by Jamila "Mia" Leonard

Code Breaker by Brian Aspinall

The Complete EdTech Coach by Katherine Goyette and Adam Juarez

Control Alt Achieve by Eric Curts

The Esports Education Playbook by Chris Aviles, Steve Isaacs,
    Christine Lion-Bailey, and Jesse Lubinsky

Google Apps for Littles by Christine Pinto and Alice Keeler

Master the Media by Julie Smith

Raising Digital Leaders by Jennifer Casa-Todd

Reality Bytes by Christine Lion-Bailey, Jesse Lubinsky, and
    Micah Shippee, PhD

Sail the 7 Cs with Microsoft Education by Becky Keene and
    Kathi Kersznowski

Shake Up Learning by Kasey Bell

Social LEADia by Jennifer Casa-Todd

Stepping Up to Google Classroom by Alice Keeler and
    Kimberly Mattina

Teaching Math with Google Apps by Alice Keeler and
    Diana Herrington

Teachingland by Amanda Fox and Mary Ellen Weeks

Teaching with Google Jamboard by Alice Keeler and Kimberly Mattina

Teaching Methods & Materials

All 4s and 5s by Andrew Sharos

Boredom Busters by Katie Powell

The Classroom Chef by John Stevens and Matt Vaudrey

The Collaborative Classroom by Trevor Muir

Copyrighteous by Diana Gill

CREATE by Bethany J. Petty

Deploying EduProtocols by Kim Voge, with Jon Corippo and
    Marlena Hebern
Ditch That Homework by Matt Miller and Alice Keeler
Ditch That Textbook by Matt Miller
Don't Ditch That Tech by Matt Miller, Nate Ridgway, and
    Angelia Ridgway
EDrenaline Rush by John Meehan
Educated by Design by Michael Cohen, The Tech Rabbi
The EduProtocol Field Guide by Marlena Hebern and Jon Corippo
The EduProtocol Field Guide: Book 2 by Marlena Hebern and
    Jon Corippo
The EduProtocol Field Guide: Math Edition by Lisa Nowakowski and
    Jeremiah Ruesch
Expedition Science by Becky Schnekser
Frustration Busters by Katie Powell
Fully Engaged by Michael Matera and John Meehan
Game On? Brain On! by Lindsay Portnoy, PhD
Guided Math AMPED by Reagan Tunstall
Innovating Play by Jessica LaBar-Twomy and Christine Pinto
Instructional Coaching Connection by Nathan Lang-Raad
Instant Relevance by Denis Sheeran
Keeping the Wonder by Jenna Copper, Ashley Bible, Abby Gross, and
    Staci Lamb
LAUNCH by John Spencer and A.J. Juliani
Make Learning MAGICAL by Tisha Richmond
Pass the Baton by Kathryn Finch and Theresa Hoover
Project-Based Learning Anywhere by Lori Elliott
Pure Genius by Don Wettrick
The Revolution by Darren Ellwein and Derek McCoy
Shift This! by Joy Kirr
Skyrocket Your Teacher Coaching by Michael Cary Sonbert
Spark Learning by Ramsey Musallam
Sparks in the Dark by Travis Crowder and Todd Nesloney
Table Talk Math by John Stevens
Unpack Your Impact by Naomi O'Brien and LaNesha Tabb

The Wild Card by Hope and Wade King
Writefully Empowered by Jacob Chastain
The Writing on the Classroom Wall by Steve Wyborney
You Are Poetry by Mike Johnston

Inspiration, Professional Growth & Personal Development

Be REAL by Tara Martin
Be the One for Kids by Ryan Sheehy
The Coach ADVenture by Amy Illingworth
Creatively Productive by Lisa Johnson
Educational Eye Exam by Alicia Ray
The EduNinja Mindset by Jennifer Burdis
Empower Our Girls by Lynmara Colón and Adam Welcome
Finding Lifelines by Andrew Grieve and Andrew Sharos
The Four O'Clock Faculty by Rich Czyz
How Much Water Do We Have? by Pete and Kris Nunweiler
P Is for Pirate by Dave and Shelley Burgess
A Passion for Kindness by Tamara Letter
The Path to Serendipity by Allyson Apsey
Rogue Leader by Rich Czyz
Sanctuaries by Dan Tricarico
Saving Sycamore by Molly B. Hudgens
The SECRET SAUCE by Rich Czyz
Shattering the Perfect Teacher Myth by Aaron Hogan
Stories from Webb by Todd Nesloney
Talk to Me by Kim Bearden
Teach Better by Chad Ostrowski, Tiffany Ott, Rae Hughart, and
    Jeff Gargas
Teach Me, Teacher by Jacob Chastain
Teach, Play, Learn! by Adam Peterson
The Teachers of Oz by Herbie Raad and Nathan Lang-Raad
TeamMakers by Laura Robb and Evan Robb
Through the Lens of Serendipity by Allyson Apsey
The Zen Teacher by Dan Tricarico

Children's Books

Beyond Us by Aaron Polansky

Cannonball In by Tara Martin

Dolphins in Trees by Aaron Polansky

I Can Achieve Anything by MoNique Waters

I Want to Be a Lot by Ashley Savage

The Princes of Serendip by Allyson Apsey

Ride with Emilio by Richard Nares

The Wild Card Kids by Hope and Wade King

Zom-Be a Design Thinker by Amanda Fox